# Color AND Composition

## FOR THE CREATIVE QUILTER

**IMPROVE ANY QUILT WITH EASY-TO-FOLLOW LESSONS**

# KATIE PASQUINI MASOPUST AND BRETT BARKER

C&T PUBLISHING

Publisher: Amy Marson
Editorial Director: Gailen Runge
Acquisitions Editor: Jan Grigsby
Editor: Lynn Koolish
Technical Editors: Joyce Lytle and Robyn Gronning
Copyeditor/Proofreader: Randi Perkins, Glo Cantwell,
Wordfirm, Inc.
Cover Designer: Christina D. Jarumay
Book Designer/Design Director: Christina D. Jarumay
Illustrator: Brett Barker and Tim Manibusan
Production Assistant: Tim Manibusan
Photography: Luke Mulks unless otherwise noted
Published by C&T Publishing, Inc., P.O. Box 1456,
Lafayette, CA 94549
Front cover: *Big Leaves* by Katie Pasquini Masopust, photo by
Hawthorne Studio
Back cover: *Tesque Aspens* by Brett Barker, photo by Hawthorne
Studio; *Birch Trees* by Ree Nancarrow, photo by Ree Nancarrow;
*Forest Floor* by Jan Myers-Newbury photo by Sam Newbury.

**Library of Congress Cataloging-in-Publication Data**

Pasquini Masopust, Katie.
  Color and composition for the creative quilter : improve any quilt
with easy-to-follow lessons / Katie Pasquini Masopust and Brett
Barker.
    p. cm.
  Includes index.
  ISBN 1-57120-272-2 (paper trade)
  1. Quilts--Design. 2. Quilting. 3. Color in textile crafts. I.
Barker, Brett, II. Title.

TT835.P3519 2005
746.46--dc22
                                    2005001151

Printed in China
10  9  8  7  6  5  4  3

# DEDICATION

We dedicate this book
to our students who
consistently inspire us.

# ACKNOWLEDGMENTS

We thank our word artists,
Randi and Glo.

We also thank our families,
who have always supported us.

# PREFACE

*Brett:* In the fall of 2000, I received a phone call. The nice-sounding woman on the line explained that although she was a "pretty famous" quilter (what an understatement!), she wanted to take classes from me to strengthen her skills and learn some new teaching techniques. I readily agreed. Thus began my friendship with Katie Pasquini. Katie rapidly became one of my favorite students— talented, always eager, and enthusiastic.

*Katie:* Our friendship evolved as we consulted as peers and colleagues. I loved taking classes with Brett. I enjoyed working with what were new materials for me: chalk pastels and acrylic paints.

*Brett:* We wondered whether we could reach more quilters, teaching them the "art" of art quilting. Katie had been mulling over a new book based on one of her most successful classes; I had been teaching fine art concepts through my business, Sun Studios Creativity Center. These two ideas came together, and we both decided that an art book for quilters would be a great idea!

*Katie:* As the book has grown, so has our friendship—we have learned so much from each other. We hope you enjoy the book, and, more importantly, we hope that the "art" of art quilting is now accessible to every fabric artist.

# CONTENTS

# How to Use This Book

The key to this book is practice. You can read the directions and understand the rationale, but if you don't do the exercises, sometimes over and over again, the concepts won't be ingrained into your psyche and soul. As Goethe said, "Begin, and the work will be completed." To increase your artistry, you must **do** the exercises. We have designed this book to be used—it is driven by practice, not theory; the theory that is included is offered only as an explanation of the exercises. Start at the beginning, and work your way through the lessons and exercises.

Creativity is nebulous, but the one thing we absolutely know is that the discipline of **practice** will increase your mastery. The path to creativity is different for each person. Just as writers (and other creative people) use daily journaling as a path to mastery, you can use this book and its exercises to access and increase your creativity. In it we describe our most successful ways of getting to a more creative place through studio setup, materials, and color and composition exercises. These exercises will allow you to discover your own unique style, so you can create beautiful, original art quilts. In each chapter, you'll see student exercises and quilts by professionals to see how they use color and composition.

At the end of the book, you can read about the positive and negative experiences quilt artists have had along their own creative pathways.

Many quilters we have talked to say they don't think about composition or color beforehand; they simply start making a quilt and *voilà!* It's wonderful. However, upon further questioning, we have noticed that these same artists either went to art school or had some sort of formal training in color and composition. Their process became "intuitive" only later, after many years of practice. This book can become **your** art school.

Through the use of this book, you will develop a **toolbox** of methods, materials, color combinations, and compositional ideas. Each chapter will give you several new tools to put in your toolbox. At first, you'll have to think about color and composition **before** you make a piece. But once you have finished the exercises in the book, you'll be able to create more intuitively.

**Brett**

I work intuitively, but as a lifelong artist, I almost **always** think about color and composition before beginning a piece. In my quilt-like pieces, I carefully plan both color and composition beforehand to guide my viewer's eye. Because these paintings emphasize a seven-step value run, it's critical to preplan the color and value so the painting feels unified.

*Sarasvati I,* 38" x 80", by Brett Barker (acrylic painting on wood painting using a seven-step value run and vertical composition)

*New Mexico Badlands,* 19" x 25", by Brett Barker (pastel painting, diagonal composition)

*Buddha, Warm and Cool,* 38" x 80", by Brett Barker (acrylic painting on wood painting, symmetrical grid composition)

Even when I'm outdoors creating a "spontaneous" plein-air painting, I look at my view of the landscape and decide what kind of composition I can create—asymmetrical, vertical, circular, and so on. Because landscape tends to conform to the horizontal, I often try to "mix it up"—adding more diagonals, creating a radiating tree, and so forth—to make the piece more exciting. I consciously sketch out my landscape with a couple of different compositional ideas in mind; I then choose the one I like best and begin painting.

### Katie

I begin my work with the camera. Photographs are my inspiration. I take several shots of my subject and look for a strong composition. I zoom in on my subject to personalize and focus on its importance, eliminating any other distractions. I usually create several drawings from the photograph, changing each as I work. Then I determine whether the composition is as I intended it to be. If not, I make another drawing, changing it for the final

time before enlarging it to use as a full-size pattern. I then decide which color scheme will best support my vision and pull those colors from my stash. I use full value runs and stick to my plan.

*Redwood Forest,* 64" x 76", by Katie Pasquini Masopust (vertical composition)

# Getting It "Right"

## THE RIGHT SIDE OF THE BRAIN

Research has shown that the right side (or hemisphere) of the brain is responsible for the nonverbal, spatial, creative intelligence that we all have. In Western cultures, right-side activity is not seen as important—the entire educational system is based on the more-valued, left-hemisphere concepts of logic, verbal-linguistic communication, and mathematical mastery. Because of this, the right hemisphere is often completely ignored.

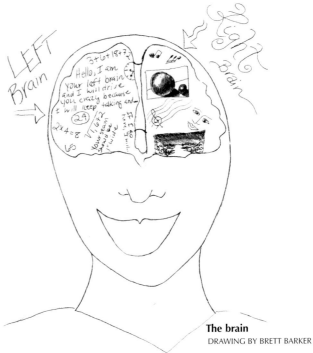

**The brain**
DRAWING BY BRETT BARKER

And yet, we all use our right side constantly—think about driving somewhere far away. As you relax on the highway, you "wake up" after a while and notice that all of a sudden, you're there! It's not that you were asleep; rather, your right side was completely engaged. You lost the sense of time and language as your right side guided you through the spatial awareness activities necessary for driving. That is just one example of the many ways in which your right brain, with its unique intelligence, helps you through each day.

Signs or signals that you are in your right brain include lost time, the inability to verbalize (it's hard to talk or listen to someone when you're in your right brain), a feeling of relaxed well-being, and **an increased ability to see visual information.**

# WHY THE RIGHT SIDE IS IMPORTANT FOR CREATIVE WORK

Have you ever heard someone say (or perhaps you've even said it yourself!), "I can't even draw a straight line!" Many people believe that only a few are born with artistic talent. That is absolutely untrue. Creativity and artistic talent **can** be learned— they are **skills** that can be **taught**. Many years of teaching these skills led us to create this book. We will show you how to use **both** your right and left sides to make great quilts with wonderful color and eye-catching compositions.

The exercises in this book are specifically targeted toward "waking up" the right side of your brain. Often, as the right side starts waking up, the left side will feel threatened. Brain research has shown that because the left-side neurons are accustomed to firing (after all, they have been in use for up to 90% of the activities throughout your life!), they literally want to stay in control. Because the left side is based in language, it will try to maintain control over your activity by sending you language-based "messages" that often take the form of negative self-talk.

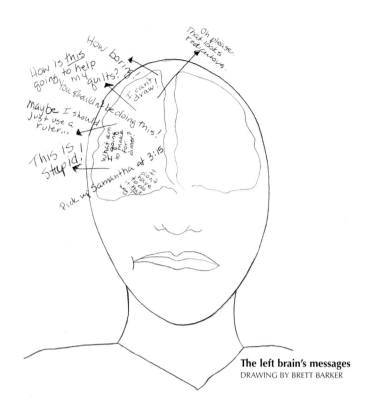

**The left brain's messages**
DRAWING BY BRETT BARKER

Messages such as "I can't do this," "This is stupid/boring/ pointless," and "I should be cutting by now" are often reported by our students when we ask their creative brains to engage.

Pay attention to these messages! Each person's left side will talk back in specific ways. Knowing what these messages are **and dismissing them** is crucial to allowing the right side to take over. When the right side finally does take over (usually after 20 minutes of sustained creative activity), you'll be able to see and work more creatively.

# MAKE YOUR RIGHT SIDE COMFORTABLE: CREATING A WORK SPACE CONDUCIVE TO CREATIVITY

There are certain parameters that **must** be respected for your right brain to thrive. You must be focused, with no outside distractions. Carving out creative time for yourself is a kind of artistic discipline. We are not talking about a negative, harsh discipline, but rather the joyous discipline of knowing you have the time and space for creative flow.

Go into your studio or work area free of left-brain distractions. You need to have an organized space of your own in which to work. We're not talking immaculate; however, you do need to know where your tools are, what fabrics are to be cut, and so on, so you can perform these right-brained tasks without having to think (i.e., use your left brain). Sort fabrics by color and value steps so you can easily select them.

Scissors and rotary cutters should be sharp so you can cut fabric without frustration. Make sure that your sewing machine is well maintained and in good working order so you won't spend your valuable artistic time working out mechanical problems. Ideally your studio should be used for only one thing, the making of your art. Not everyone has a separate space in which to work, but whatever space you have should be organized and treated with respect. Any time spent organizing will be rewarded later, as your right brain can then engage more easily.

Certain kinds of music aid right-brain activity. Instrumental music is the most conducive to right-brain activity. The words (lyrics) in music are often heard subconsciously by your left, or verbal, brain, keeping you from reaching your creative space. As you turn on music, turn off the phone! Nothing catapults you back into your left brain faster than the jarring sound of a ringing telephone.

Well-meaning friends and family will often interrupt when you are in your studio. Having respect for your creative work means explaining that time spent in your   studio is sacrosanct. Nothing short of a true emergency should interrupt **your** time. This can initially be a challenge. However, by making the time and space for your right-brained, creative work, you, and everyone around you, will benefit.

**Katie's right-brained studio**

# Materials AND **Methods**

## MATERIALS

Here's what you'll need to do the exercises in the book.

### Art Tools

- Pencil
- 8$\frac{1}{2}$" x 11" copy paper for copying and drawing
- Tracing paper
- Photocopier (or access to one)
- Magazine or other pictures, as needed
- Fruit for still life
- Lamp to light still-life arrangements
- Timer
- *The Nine-Patch of Compositions* and *The Nine-Patch of Color Schemes* (see pages 11 and 15)

Art tools

### Cutting Tools

- Scissors
- Rotary cutter
- Rotary cutting ruler
- Rotary cutting mat

Cutting tools

### Fabric Tools

- Array of fabrics: See each chapter for specific fabric requirements
- White fabric for background foundations, cut to 8$\frac{1}{2}$" x 11"
- Paper-backed fusible web of your choice
- Thin batting
- Iron and ironing surface

**Fabric tools**

## ■ Sewing Tools

- Dark sewing thread
- Sewing machine with a free-motion straight and zigzag stitch

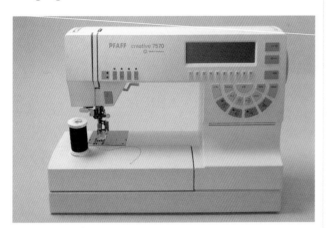
**Sewing tools**

# METHODS

## ■ Fusing

You will use fused fabrics for most of the exercises. Use a paper-backed fusible product of your choice. Cut the fabrics and the fusible into 8¹/₂" x 11" rectangles, and follow the manufacturer's instructions for ironing the fusible to the back of the fabric. It's much easier to work with pieces of fabric that are fused and ready to go. Leave the paper backing on the fabric until you are ready to use it.

## ■ Simplifying

Often, you will be asked to **simplify** when drawing. This means drawing the elements in a simpler form, eliminating details. For example, you could draw a grouping of flowers as one shape rather than as individual flowers.

**Original photo**

**Detailed drawing**

**Simplified drawing**

## Enlarging

Several of the exercises require you to **enlarge** your drawings. Enlarging can be done by using a copy machine or by using your drawing skills and the contour drawing method (see pages 16–18) to enlarge by hand. Use the method that is easiest for you.

## Making Templates

In a few of the exercises, you'll use the enlarged drawings as templates. It is important that you cut out the paper templates and then flip them over to draw around them on the paper backing of the fused fabrics. It is frustrating when you forget to flip over the template and end up cutting the fabrics incorrectly; therefore, the words **cut, flip, trace,** and **place** will be in bold to help you remember these steps.

## Subject Matter

We have designed each chapter using different subject matter (florals, architecture, nonrepresentational designs, and so on). However, you may exchange the subject matter of any exercise to suit yourself.

Photocopy the *Nine-Patch of Compositions* so you can keep it in front of you while working on all of the exercises.

# COMPOSITION

The simplest definition of composition is "the arrangement of line, shape, and color to create a harmonious whole." This definition can apply to any visual artwork: a quilt, a painting, or even a sculpture. Composition is an often-overlooked aspect of effective art quilting. A good composition shows the viewer where and how the eye should move through a piece. No amount of gorgeous color, stitching, or embellishment can overcome a bad composition. The exercises in this book are based on tried-and-true compositional principles; working through these exercises will give you the confidence to easily create great quilts.

## The Nine-Patch of Compositions

Of the many compositional arrangements available, we have chosen nine that can be used to create beautiful art quilts. We call these *The Nine-Patch of Compositions.* You will be using this *Nine-Patch* tool throughout the book. Although you might wish to combine compositions, try to adhere to one dominant compositional arrangement in each exercise. Go easy on yourself and stick to just one.

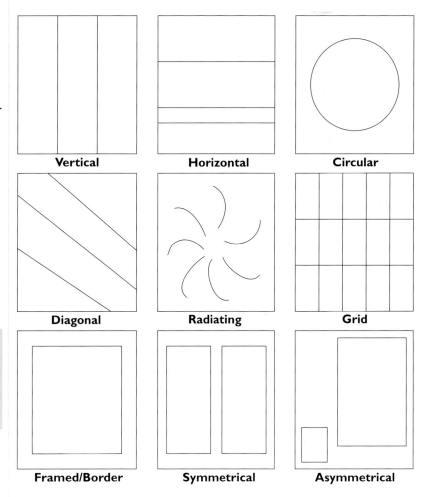

| Vertical | Horizontal | Circular |
| Diagonal | Radiating | Grid |
| Framed/Border | Symmetrical | Asymmetrical |

*The Nine-Patch of Compositions*

## ■ Composition Examples

PHOTO BY GREGORY GANTNER

***Resurrection,*** 28¹/₂" x 42", by Jane A. Sassaman

CIRCULAR

PHOTO BY PHI INC.

***Coriolis,*** 69" x 58", by Judy B. Dales

PHOTO BY REE NANCARROW

HORIZONTAL

***Moods of McKinley,***
69" x 43",
by Ree Nancarrow

## FRAMED/BORDER

*The Future Is Open,*
45" x 54",
by Denise Labadie

## SYMMETRICAL

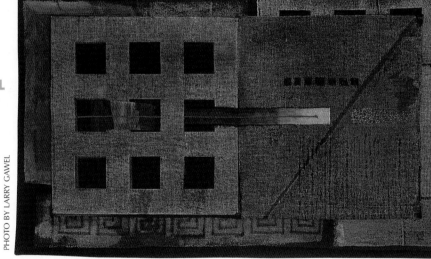

*Penumbra,* 28" x 16 1/2", by Judy James

## ASYMMETRICAL

*Time Transshifting,*
25 1/2" x 20",
by Carol Shinn

**DIAGONAL**

***Sweet Spring,*** 52" x 36", by Jan Myers-Newbury

**RADIATING**

***Flower Arrangement VI,*** 34" x 34", by Sue Benner

**GRID**

***Beyond Mora,*** 40" x 60", by John Garrett

## ■ The Nine-Patch of Color Schemes

Color is another tool in your art quilter's toolbox. Effective use of color can reinforce a composition and help clarify your intention. Ineffective use of color can make a good quilt mediocre in a hurry. With that in mind, we have designed exercises to help you understand color theory. From the numerous color schemes available, we have again chosen nine, *The Nine-Patch of Color Schemes*.

**Fabric color wheel**

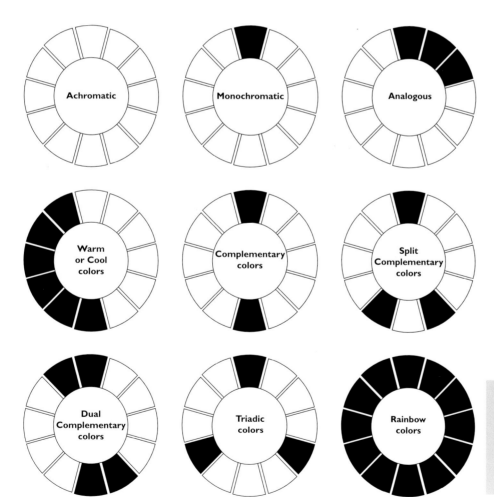

*The Nine-Patch of Color Schemes*

Photocopy the *Nine-Patch of Color Schemes* so you can keep it in front of you while working on all of the exercises.

# Contour Drawing

Contour refers to the lines that make up the exteriors and interiors of an object. Contour drawing is a line drawing with no shading. This type of drawing stimulates your right brain, allowing you to see objects exactly as they appear.

## EXERCISE 1:
## BLIND CONTOUR DRAWING

In blind contour drawing, you draw the contours of the objects without looking at the paper as you draw. This is the first of three contour drawing exercises.

### ■ Materials
- Copy paper
- Pencil
- Still life setup of 3 fruits (some suggestions are pears, apples, bananas, or grapes)
- Timer
- Lamp for light source

### ■ Directions

1. Set up a still life of 3 different fruits. Put the lamp on one side of the still life to create highlights and shadows. You may choose to cut the fruit, exposing the often complex and interesting interiors. Place the still life on a white piece of paper to eliminate distractions.

**Typical still life setup**

2. Draw a frame around the edges of your paper, leaving about a 1" margin on all sides. Do **not** use a ruler! A ruler is a left-brained tool, and you are accessing your right brain in this exercise

**Draw a frame.**

3. Shield your view of the still life with a piece of paper.

**4.** Set the timer for 25 minutes. Draw the contours of your still life **without** looking at your paper **at all** for 25 minutes. Look carefully only at the objects, and draw **slowly**. Move your pencil in unison with the movement of your eye, over and around the **edges** of the shapes you see. They are no longer fruits; they are simply shapes and edges. Your edge may start at one fruit and continue through and over other fruits before your line stops. Don't listen to your left brain labeling each portion of the drawing that you are working on—"an apple" or "this part of the banana." Instead, simply focus on the shapes that you see without labeling them. Your right brain might use nonjudgmental words, such as "I am now going over this curve" or "this part is now going up." That is to be encouraged.

For most people, not looking at a drawing while creating it causes a sudden sense of panic; that feeling is simply your left brain trying desperately to stay in control. The irony is that while your right brain really **loves** this kind of project, your left brain will often protest. Don't let that bother you. Remember to hold a separate piece of paper as a shield above your drawing so you can't see what you're doing. It may help if you turn your chair away. Don't peek! Every time you peek, you put your left brain back in control. You may even find that in drawing, you have gone off the edge of your paper—that is a positive indication that your right brain is completely engaged.

If you have trouble, move your fingers close to the eraser end of the pencil. Drawing often creates tension in the body; moving your fingers to the eraser end of the pencil will make you feel more relaxed. Do not shade; just draw the contours. Keep at it for the full 25 minutes, until the timer goes off. (It takes the average person 20 minutes of **sustained** drawing to move from the left brain to the right.)

If your pencil starts to travel rapidly, your left brain is trying to take over. A great way to make your right brain re-engage is to **slow down!** Your eye and pencil should literally be moving along together at a snail's pace. Follow the advice on page 8—play some music, take the phone off the hook, **relax!** Practice ignoring the negative self-talk that your left brain will try to engage in.

Because this process is blind, your drawing may not look **at all** like the still life. However, once your time is up, if you look closely, you'll see that the quality of the line is very detailed and often beautiful. Your lines should not be smooth—when you create a smooth line, your left brain has decided to go faster "to help you"! Your right brain will want to go slowly, drawing every little nuance. Your left brain simply cannot make up such convoluted, complex lines—only your relaxed, right brain can truly **see** these lines so you can **draw** them.

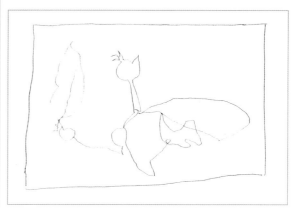

**Still life, blind-contour drawing by Sue Kongs**

PHOTO BY KATIE PASQUINI MASOPUST

**Sue Kongs shields her drawing.**

# EXERCISE 2:
## SEMI-BLIND, OR MODIFIED, CONTOUR DRAWING

When you look at your paper for only a small portion of the time you are drawing, you are creating a semi-blind, or modified, contour drawing. This is the next step in the contour drawing process.

### ■ Directions

1. Repeat the drawing process on a new sheet of paper. This time, you may look at your paper to begin the contour of a new object or to ensure that you haven't gone off the edge. However, when you look at your drawing, stop the motion of your pencil. Your goal is to fill the entire frame with a large drawing by drawing and looking at the still life 75% of the time and stopping the action of your pencil to look at the drawing only 25% of the time.

2. Don't forget to set your timer for 25 minutes. The timer allows your right brain to engage more quickly. Watching the clock is a left-brain activity; by setting the timer, you take away that left-brain interruption.

**Still life, modified contour drawing** by Sue Kongs

# EXERCISE 3:
## CONTOUR DRAWING

In this contour drawing exercise, keep the attitude of blind and semi-blind drawing by focusing on your objects more than on your paper, even though you can look at your paper more than in the previous exercises. (You can use contour drawing to enlarge your drawings in future exercises.)

### ■ Directions

Draw the same still life again for 25 minutes. This time you can look at your paper as often as you like, but keep in mind that the more you look at the still life and **not** at your paper, the more you are engaging your right brain. Check your paper only once in a while for accurate placement. The rest of the time, the bulk of the time, should be spent **seeing** your still life.

**Still life, contour drawing** by Sue Kongs

You can do these three exercises all in one day or for 25 minutes a day for three days in a row, whichever works best for you.

## The Why Box

Compare your first drawing with your last. Your lines have probably become much more complex and expressive as you have learned to truly **see** objects the way they are, versus how your left brain "thinks" they should be. You may not be pleased with the results of your blind and semi-blind drawings. **That is okay!** You are training your right brain to engage more easily, and that training, **not your drawing**, is the most important part of the exercise.

To keep your right brain active, practice contour drawing in place of, or along with, journaling, daily. Take a quiet moment, set up a still life or pick an area of your room, and draw. The more you draw, the more comfortable it will become, and the faster the creative ideas will flow.

**Apple With a View,** 26" x 43", student quilt by Sue Kongs (asymmetrical composition)

**Drawing for quilt** by Sue Kongs

**Blind contour drawing** by Marie Longserre

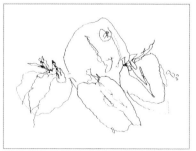

**Modified contour drawing** by Marie Longserre

**Contour drawing** by Marie Longserre

# Contour Cutting
## AND Stitching

Contour cutting translates the concepts of contour drawing (see pages 16–19) to fabrics and sewing.

## EXERCISE 1: CONTOUR CUTTING A REALISTIC DESIGN

Contour cutting is similar to contour drawing except that you use a pair of scissors instead of a pencil to define the contours of the objects. The cut shapes will then be arranged to create a realistic design.

### ■ Materials
- Fused fabrics in a variety of colors that are representational of the fruits in your still life
- Gray fabric: 2 pieces 8$\frac{1}{2}$" x 11" for background foundation
- Iron
- Still life from the previous chapter (You may need fresh fruit!)
- Lamp for a light source

### ■ Directions
1. Set up the still life and light source as you did for the previous chapter.

**Still life setup**

**NOTE:** In Steps 3–4 you will cut 2 sets of fabric shapes: 1 set for this exercise and 1 set for Exercise 2. For each shape you cut, place 1 piece of fabric on top of another (both pieces should be right side up) so you cut both at the same time.

2. Take the time to really look at the fruit. Observe the highlights and shadows that are present.

3. Remove the paper backing from the fused fabrics. Place 2 pieces of fabric together as noted. Use your scissors as you did your pencil, cutting along the edge of your fruit in a modified contour fashion, looking at your scissors and fabric only 25% of the time. As you did in contour drawing, look mainly at the fruit, not at the fabric. The speed of your scissors should equal the previously slow speed of your pencil.

**Contour cutting**

**4.** After the fruit shapes are cut, choose fabrics that match the highlights on the fruit, and cut out 2 of each shape in the same modified contour fashion. Remember to use your scissors as a pencil; don't draw on the fabric.

**Apple shapes with highlights**

**5.** Look at the shadows of the still life, and cut those out, using dark fabric for each shadow shape. Black may not be your best choice for shadows; it is often too dark in comparison with the fruit. A gray or a darker value of the fruit's color may be a better choice. (See pages 31–33 for more on value.)

**Apple shapes with highlights and shadows**

**6.** You now have 2 identical sets of fabric shapes. Separate the shapes into 2 equal stacks. One set will be used for this exercise; the other will be saved for the next.

**7.** Arrange 1 set of shapes on the gray fabric to make a realistic still life. Because templates are not used, the shapes will not line up perfectly. They don't need to be perfect. Fuse the pieces in place.

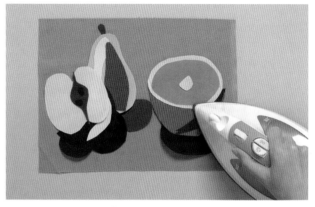

**Shapes do not need to line up perfectly.**

**Realistic still life**
by Sue Kongs

**Realistic still life**
by Cindy Barfield

## The Why Box

*In creating this still life, you rely on your right brain, taking your time to cut the shapes in a modified contour fashion. You learn how to translate your drawing skills to fabric, seeing the still life as it truly is. If you have always used templates, you may find that this way of working is spontaneous, free, and exciting!*

# EXERCISE 2:
## CONTOUR CUTTING AN ABSTRACT DESIGN

Abstraction means making something real (in this case, a still life) look less real by rearranging elements according to a compositional choice. Creating a simple, abstract design is the first step in becoming familiar with *The Nine-Patch of Compositions.*

### ■ Directions

**1.** Choose a *Nine-Patch* compositional arrangement (see page 11). Arrange the second set of shapes from Exercise 1 according to your chosen composition, so that it appears strongly circular, diagonal, and so forth.

**2.** Test your compositional choice by asking a friend to determine the arrangement you selected. If your friend sees a different composition than you intended, change a few elements to make your composition more obvious. Fuse the shapes in place.

**Abstract radiating composition** by Sue Kongs

**Abstract radiating composition** by Cindy Barfield

### ■ STILL LIFE QUILTS

*Rich and Zesty,* 30" x 10", by B. J. Adams (horizontal composition)

PHOTO BY PAUL-RICARDO S. ELBO

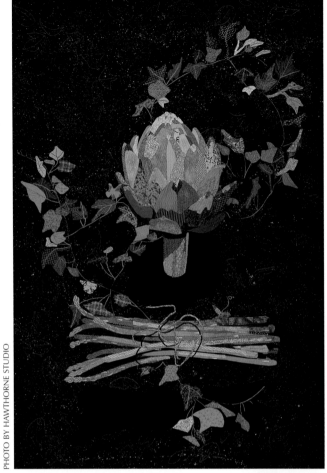

PHOTO BY HAWTHORNE STUDIO

*Artichoke, Asparagus, and a Side of Ivy,*
32" x 45", by Katie Pasquini Masopust
(vertical composition)

PHOTO BY MARK GULEZIAN/QUICKSILVER

*Stills From a Life 2,*
60" x 40$\frac{1}{2}$",
by Dominie Nash
(diagonal composition)

*The Why Box*

When you make elements conform solely to a compositional
idea, bypassing a realistic
depiction, you create a piece
that is abstract. Abstraction
allows you to play with color,
value, and shape without wor-
rying about whether your piece
looks real. Try placing realistic
shapes in an abstract fashion to
make a unique art quilt.

PHOTO BY SHARON RISEDORPH

*Crimson Delight,*
58" x 42$\frac{3}{4}$",
by Yvonne Porcella
(framed composition)

# EXERCISE 3: FREE-MOTION CONTOUR STITCHING

For contour stitching, treat your machine just as you did the pencil and scissors in the previous exercises. Look mainly at your still life and only occasionally at the needle. This technique results in a modified-contour, free-motion rendering of the still life. This piece will **not** look photo-realistic! Remember, you are looking for the quality of the line created with your machine.

## ■ Materials

- White fabric: 2 squares 10" x 10"
- Batting: 1 square 10" x 10"
- Spray baste
- Dark thread
- Sewing machine
- Same still life used in Exercises 1 and 2

## ■ Directions

1. Spray the batting with spray baste, and smooth a piece of white fabric over each side to create a fabric sandwich.

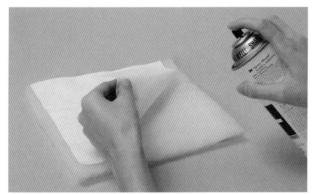

**Use spray baste to create fabric sandwich.**

2. Thread your sewing machine with dark thread in both bobbin and top. (Be sure the bobbin is full; stopping to refill a bobbin throws you back into your left brain.) Looking at the still life, free-motion sew **without drawing any lines on the fabric beforehand.** You **are** allowed to look at your fabric and machine (we don't want you to sew over your fingers).

PHOTO BY KATIE PASQUINI MASOPUST

**Brett Barker free-motion quilting**

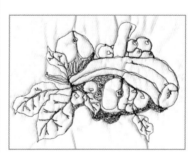

**Realistic still life** by Dawn Siden

**Realistic still life** by Cheryl Philips

# OPTIONAL EXERCISE

Return to the realistic still life and the abstraction pieces from page 20–22. Layer and free-motion machine quilt those as well; use the blind contour stitching technique to add complexity. Notice how the stitching creates a more finished look.

**Diagonal abstraction** by Katie Pasquini Masopust

**Realistic still life** by Katie Pasquini Masopust

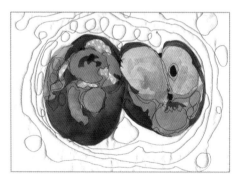

**Realistic still life** by Shelley Longmire

**Realistic still life** by Lorrie Bonds Lopez

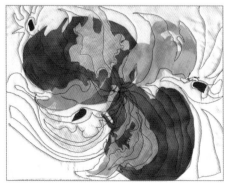

**Radiating abstraction** by Shelley Longmire

## The Why Box

You will be amazed at the beauty of this free-motion quilting! You are learning to really **see** without left-brain judgment—a **big** step in the process of becoming more artistic! This will enable you to freely machine quilt your pieces without relying on a drawn line or a pattern.

# Line AND Shape

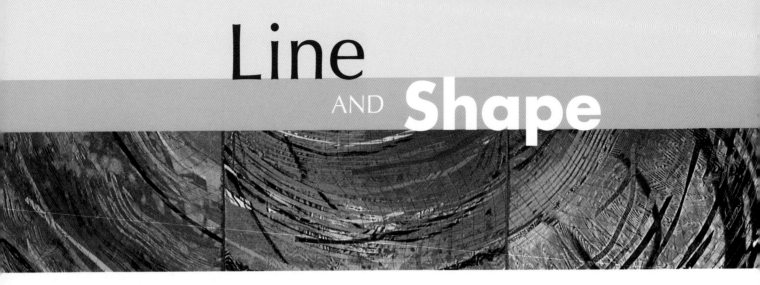

Creating designs with simplified lines and shapes is the first step in effectively using *The Nine-Patch of Compositions*. Line and shape are used to create a balance between positive shapes (lines, squares, and so on) and negative spaces (the air or white space of the background).

## EXERCISE 1: COMPOSING WITH LINE

A fabric **line** is created when the strip of fabric is longer than it is wide. Use fabric strips (lines) to create four different composition arrangements.

### Materials
- Fused black fabric: 2 pieces 8¹/₂" x 11"
- White fabric: 4 pieces 8¹/₂" x 11" for background foundations
- Rotary cutting ruler
- Rotary cutter
- Cutting mat
- Iron

### Directions
1. Remove the paper backing from the fused fabric. Cut strips of black fused fabric. All strips should be at least 11" long and of varying widths.

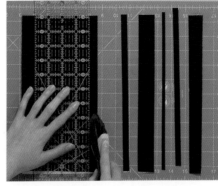

Cut strips 11" long with varying widths.

2. Choose a composition from *The Nine-Patch of Compositions*. Use the black strips to create that composition on a piece of white fabric. Place the strips so that all lines are parallel to the edges of the foundation. You can cut the strips to meet your needs. The white space is the negative space, and the black lines are the positive. Break up the white negative space using black positive strips. Overlapping is okay, but not necessary. Save the leftover strips for Step 4.

3. Fuse the strips in place.

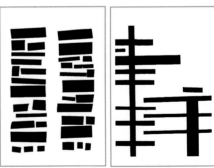

**Symmetrical composition**
by Linda Pysto

**Asymmetrical composition**
by Cheryl Phillips

**4.** Choose a second *Nine-Patch* composition. Use the leftover strips to create a second composition. This time, break up the negative space with diagonal lines, cutting additional straight strips if necessary. In this composition, none of the lines will be parallel to the edge of the foundation.

**5.** Fuse the strips in place.

**Circular composition** by Doris Koozer

**Diagonal composition**
by Katie Pasquini Masopust

**6.** Cut curved strips of varying widths and lengths; make sure that even though curved, these pieces look like thick lines rather than shapes. Create a third composition from *The Nine-Patch of Compositions.* using your curved strips.

**7.** Fuse the strips in place.

**Asymmetrical composition**
by Vinda Robison

**Radiating composition** by Sharon Signorelli

**Grid composition** by Muriel Funka

**8.** Combine any or all of the previous strips, curved and straight, to create a fourth composition of your choice.

**9.** Fuse the strips in place.

**Framed composition** by Doris Koozer

**Asymmetrical composition**
by Rebecca Chapin

This exercise adapted from Design *principles and Problems* 1st Edition by Zelanski, published by Wadsworth © 1984 ISBN:0030511666.

The Why Box

*Using strips is a good way to create compositions in a fast, free manner. The extreme value change of black and white allows you to easily see the positive and negative relationships.*

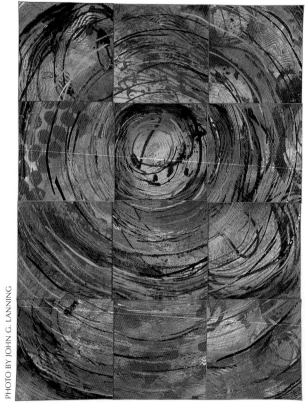

**Nest I,**
46$^1/_2$" x 62",
by Sue Benner
(circular composition)

**Cast Party,** 28" x 22",
acrylic painting by Ned Wert
(horizontal composition)

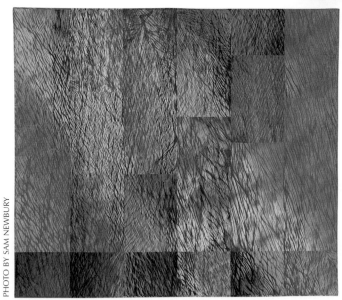

**Forest Floor,**
72$^1/_2$" x 61",
by Jan Myers-Newbury
(grid composition)

# EXERCISE 2: COMPOSING WITH SHAPE

Use shape and a focal point to create a composition.

## ▨ Materials

- Fused fabric in 2 different colors: 2 pieces of each color
- White fabric: 2 pieces 8¹/₂" x 11" for background foundations
- Rotary cutting ruler
- Rotary cutter
- Cutting mat
- Iron

## ▨ Directions

**1.** Remove the paper backing from the fused fabric, and cut 16 shapes of 1 color, as follows:

   6 squares 1" x 1"
   6 squares 2" x 2"
   2 squares 4" x 4"
   2 rectangles 1" x 4"

Separate the shapes into 2 equal sets. Put a set aside.

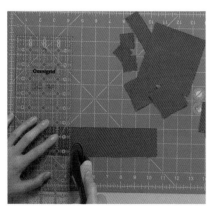

**Cut shapes.**

**2.** Choose a composition from *The Nine-Patch of Compositions.* Use a set of shapes from Step 1 and place them on the white fabric to create the composition you selected.

It's helpful to ask someone else to look at *The Nine-Patch of Compositions* chart and tell you which composition you created. If your intention isn't clear, try again.

**3.** After you have successfully created your composition, fuse the squares to the fabric.

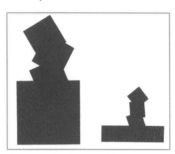

**Asymmetrical composition**
by Linda Eslinger

**Diagonal composition** by Ann Malone

**Vertical composition** by Brett Barker

**4.** Cut 1 square 2" x 2" from the second color. Choose another composition from *The Nine-Patch of Compositions,* and make a new composition on the second piece of white fabric using the second stack of shapes from Step 1 **and** the new 2" square as the focal point.

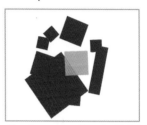

**Circular composition** by Deb Martin

**Diagonal composition** by Joyce Reed

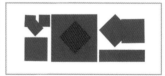

**Horizontal composition** by Linda Eslinger

## The Why Box

*Sometimes one different colored square will emphasize your compositional choice, and sometimes it will detract from it. Keep that concept in mind as you create a quilt—do different colors emphasize your choices or do they detract from your intention?*

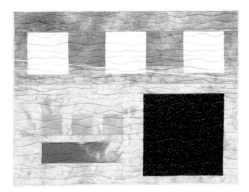

***Untitled,*** 33" x 25", student quilt
by Sharon Signorelli
(horizontal composition)

PHOTO BY D. MICHAEL McCORMICK

***First Light,*** 58½" x 68", by Judy B. Dales
(grid composition)

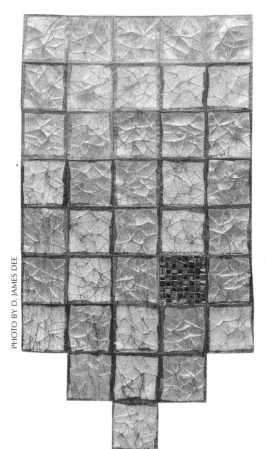

PHOTO BY D. JAMES DEE

***Window,*** 30" x 54", by Patricia Malarcher
(grid composition)

PHOTO BY JUDY SMITH KRESSLEY

***Autumn Improv,*** 48" x 40", by Gabrielle Swain
(grid composition)

# Value
## AND Color

**V**alue is the most important aspect of color. A full range of values, from light to dark, makes the difference between a mediocre quilt and a true piece of art. Usually the very lights and the deepest darks are forgotten. Because lighter colors can illuminate a quilt and darks can add depth and richness, we encourage the use of a **seven-step** value run in art pieces.

## EXERCISE 1: GRAY-SCALE VALUE RUN

This arrangement of gray values is one of the most important tools you can possess as an art quilter. It will help you evaluate each color's value.

### ■ Materials
- Fused fabrics in a seven-step value run from white through grays to black
- Medium gray fabric: 1 square 18" x 18" for background foundation
- Rotary cutting ruler
- Rotary cutter
- Cutting mat
- Iron

### ■ Directions
**1.** Evaluate your fabrics to produce 7 gradations that transition smoothly in even steps from white as Value 1 to black as Value 7.

**2.** Cut 1 square 2" x 2" from each of the selected fabrics.

**3.** Remove the paper backing from the fused fabric, and place your 2" squares in order, from light to dark, on the left edge of the gray fabric. Put the light square at the top and the dark at the bottom.

**4.** Fuse the squares in place.

**Gray-scale value run**

# EXERCISE 2: GRAPHIC GRAY-SCALE

You'll add energy and vibration to the gray scale by using black-and-white graphic prints.

## ■ Materials

- Fused fabrics in black-and-white prints in a seven-step value run (Your fabrics need to be true black-and-white prints—no creams, grays, or solids.)
- Rotary cutting ruler
- Rotary cutter
- Cutting mat
- Iron

## ■ Directions

1. Evaluate your print fabrics to produce 7 gradations that transition smoothly:

Value 1: the lightest value—white print on white background

Value 2: white background with a little bit of black print

Value 3: white background with more black print

Value 4: equal amounts of black and white

Value 5: black background with a lot of white print

Value 6: black background with a bit of white print

Value 7: the darkest value—black print on black background

2. Cut 1 square 2" x 2" from each of the selected fabrics, remove the paper backing from the fused fabrics, and place them on the far right side of the gray foundation used in Exercise 1. The lightest value should be on the top and the darkest value at the bottom.

**Graphic gray-scale value run**

3. Fuse the squares in place.

## The Why Box

*It is important to have the seven-step value run as a full palette to work with. The solid gray scale allows you to more easily see value difference as you train your eye. The graphic gray scale shows you how to use black-and-white prints. Keep these two scales as a reference tool in your studio.*

# EXERCISE 3: COLOR WHEEL

A personal color wheel that you create from fabric gives you a much better sense of color theory than a printed color wheel that you simply purchase from an art store. Your color wheel will have 12 **medium-value** colors (sometimes called the **true hues**). The primary colors will have lighter versions, called **pastels** or **tints**, and darker versions, called **shades**.

## ■ Materials

- Fused fabric in all the following colors:
  - Yellow, light yellow, dark yellow
  - Yellow-orange
  - Orange, light orange, dark orange
  - Red-orange
  - Red, light red (pink), dark red
  - Red-violet
  - Violet, light violet, dark violet
  - Blue-violet
  - Blue, light blue, dark blue
  - Blue-green
  - Green, light green, dark green
  - Yellow-green
- Rotary cutting ruler
- Rotary cutter
- Cutting mat
- Iron

## ■ Directions

**1.** Evaluate your colors carefully—you are making a reference tool that you will use in the future. Compare your selected colors with the completed color wheel (on page 34) to make sure you have the right selection of colors. Cut 1 square 2" x 2" from each fabric you choose.

**2.** Create a color wheel in the center of the gray fabric that has the two gray scales. Start by placing the yellow, red, and blue squares in position as if on a clock: yellow at 12 o'clock, red at 4 o'clock, and blue at 8 o'clock. These three colors are the **primary** colors.

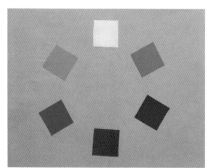

**Primaries**

**3.** Place the orange square at 2 o'clock, violet at 6 o'clock, and green at 10 o'clock. These are the **secondary** colors, the midway points between primaries.

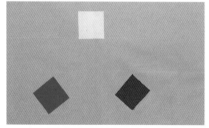

**Secondaries**

**4.** Add **tints** and **shades** to these primaries and secondaries. Place the lighter value, the tint, to the inside of each color on your wheel to make an interior ring. Place the darker values, the shades, to the outside of the medium-valued, true primaries and secondaries to make an outer ring of 6 shades.

**Tints**

**Shades**

**5.** Complete the wheel by adding the **tertiary** colors. Place the pure values of:
yellow-orange at 1 o'clock,
red-orange at 3 o'clock,
red-violet at 5 o'clock,
blue-violet at 7 o'clock,
blue-green at 9 o'clock,
and yellow-green at 11 o'clock.
See how the tertiary colors contain equal amount of the colors they are between.

**6.** Fuse the squares in place.

**Complete color wheel**

## ■ Optional Exercise

If you'd like to add tints and shades of the tertiary colors, cut out lighter-value triangles, and place them in the inner ring for the tertiary tints. Cut out darker-value 2" squares, and place them in the outer ring for the shades. Fuse the squares and triangles in place.

*The Why Box*

*Creating a color wheel and gray-scale value run tool from fabric is essential for understanding colors and value changes. The way in which color and value relate to each other is at the heart of artistic creation. Hang this tool on your wall. Use it to identify the color and value schemes used in future chapters. A fabric color wheel will help you develop your eye for color faster than any other tool in the marketplace today.*

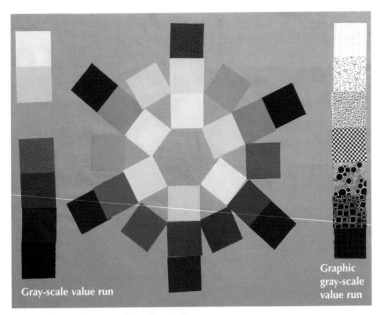

**Gray-scale value run**

**Graphic gray-scale value run**

**Color wheel and gray-scales value tool**

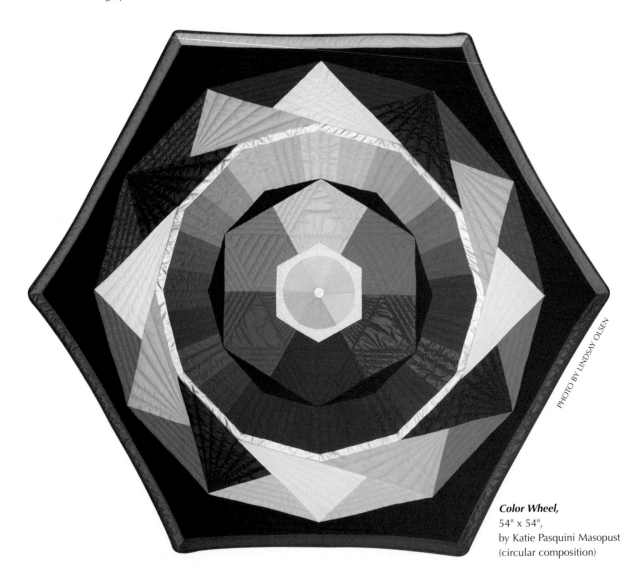

PHOTO BY LINDSAY OLSEN

***Color Wheel,***
54" x 54",
by Katie Pasquini Masopust
(circular composition)

# Monochromatic
## AND Achromatic
## Color Schemes

Monochromatic is defined as one color; achromatic is the absence of color (black and white). It is important to use the full value run when you work with only one color (or no color), being sure to include the very lightest and the darkest values.

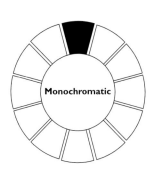

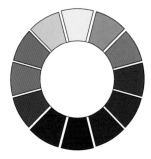

## EXERCISE 1: MONOCHROMATIC FOCAL POINT

Choose one color in a seven-step value run to create the first composition. To pick the seven value steps for this composition, you'll learn to compare color with the gray scale to assess value.

### ■ Materials

- Fused fabrics in a seven-step value run of **one** color
- White fabric: 1 piece 8½" x 11" for background foundation
- Gray scale and color wheel (see pages 31—34)
- Pencil
- Copy paper
- Iron

### ■ Directions

**1.** Pick a potential medium value 4 fabric in your chosen color. Place it next to the value 4 gray-scale square on your gray-scale tool. Squint your eyes. If you can see the line between your colored fabric and your gray fabric, the colored fabric is not the correct value. Choose and evaluate until the gray and the colored fabric blend into each other.

Now pick the 6 additional values of the same color in the same manner. Arrange these fabrics from light (value 1) to dark (value 7).

**Comparing colored fabric with a gray scale to assess value**

**Colored fabrics aligned from light to dark**

**2.** Cut a 2$^{1}$/$_{8}$" x 2$^{3}$/$_{4}$" window in the middle of a piece of blank white paper to use as a viewfinder for this and other exercises.

**3.** Return to your contour drawings (see pages 16–18). Move the viewfinder around on your drawings until you find an abstract composition that is pleasing **and** that coincides with one of the compositions of *The Nine-Patch of Compositions*. Make sure that within the viewfinder, you have a **focal point**—an interesting combination of lines that immediately attracts your attention. Tape down the viewfinder. If you don't feel your focal point is strong enough, add a few lines now.

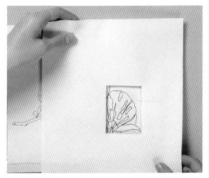
**Find the focal point with a viewfinder.**

**4.** Enlarge the design within the viewfinder by 400% to 8$^{1}$/$_{2}$" x 11". Make at least 3 copies—1 to use for templates and a couple of extras in case you lose a few pieces in the process. Trace your design onto a piece of white 8$^{1}$/$_{2}$" x 11" fabric. (If you prefer to fuse to paper, make an extra copy of your composition.)

**5.** Locate the focal point on the enlarged copy or on your white fabric foundation.

From the template copy, **cut** out the shapes for the focal point. Your focal point will alternate between value 1 and value 7 fabrics. **Flip** the template shapes over, and **trace** each shape onto the paper backing of the fused value 1 and value 7 fabrics, alternating between the two values. Cut out the shapes on the line, remove the paper backing, and **place** each shape into position on the background foundation. Continue until the focal point is complete. If you don't have enough pieces in the focal point to alternate between the light and dark fabric, add another piece now.

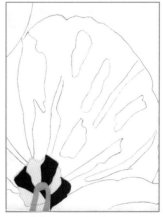
**Foundation with focal point applied**

**6.** Use the remaining fabrics (avoiding values 1 and 7) to **cut, flip, trace,** and **place** the shapes, filling in the rest of the composition. Save all the templates to use in Exercise 2. You now have a monochromatic design with a dramatic focal point.

**Radiating composition, monochromatic color scheme** by Sue Kongs

**Diagonal composition** by Donna Malabre

**Diagonal composition** by Deb Martin

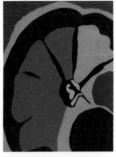
**Circular composition** by Sharon Signorelli

**Asymmetrical composition** by Carol Donachy

## ■ MONOCHROMATIC QUILTS

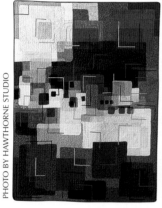

PHOTO BY HAWTHORNE STUDIO

*6 Monochromatic Quilts,*
each approximately
26" x 36",
by Katie Pasquini Masopust

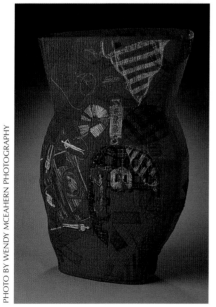

PHOTO BY WENDY MCEAHERN PHOTOGRAPHY

*The Why Box*

A monochromatic design helps you see subtle differences in value. An exciting monochromatic piece depends on a **true** seven-step value run. The contrast of the focal point adds drama.

*Carousel,*
14" x 22½" x 6",
by Kay Khan
(vertical composition)

*Eyes on the Prey,*
33" x 18", student quilt
by Venisa M. Gallegos
(grid composition)

PHOTO BY PATRICIA GOULD

***The Grand Canyon***, 40" x 60",
by Patricia Gould (asymmetrical composition)

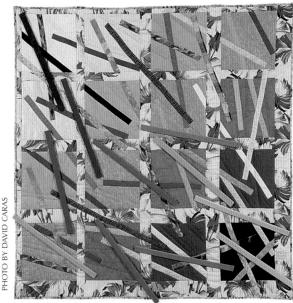

PHOTO BY DAVID CARAS

***Pick-Up Sticks,*** 51" x 51",
by Sandra Townsend Donabed (grid composition)

# EXERCISE 2: ACHROMATIC FOCAL POINT

Achromatic color schemes are literally "without color." Use black-and-white graphic prints for this exercise.

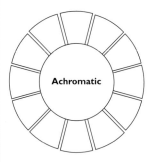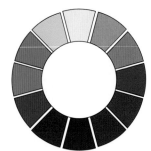

## ■ Materials

- Fused fabrics in black-and-white prints in a seven-step value run (Use your graphic gray-scale value run from the previous chapter as a guide.)
- White fabric: 1 piece 8½ " x 11" for the background foundation
- Pencil
- Copy paper
- Templates from Exercise 1
- Iron

## ■ Directions

Re-create the monochromatic design using black-and-white graphic prints by following the steps from Exercise 1. If you feel that the focal point was not strong enough in your monochromatic design, improve on it now by choosing a different spot in the same drawing.

**Radiating composition**
by Sue Kongs

# ■ ACHROMATIC QUILTS

PHOTO BY PAUL-RICARDO S. ELBO

*The Remarkables,*
36¹/₂" x 30¹/₂",
by B. J. Adams
(horizontal composition)

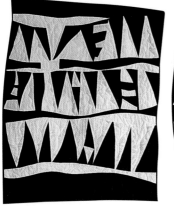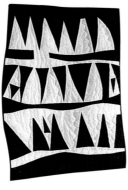

PHOTO BY MARLA HATTABAUGH

*Friv! Serious Frivolity II and III,* 32" x 39", and 26" x 34" by Marla
Hattabaugh (horizontal composition)

## The Why Box

Black-and-white quilts can be very striking.
When you work with graphic prints, the composition may seem distracting and jumbled
until you look at your piece from a distance.
You'll know you selected your values correctly
when you step back and think, WOW!

**Diagonal composition**
by Donna Malabre

**Diagonal composition**
by Deb Martin

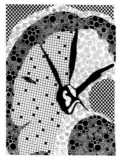

**Circular composition**
by Sharon Signorelli

**Asymmetrical composition**
by Carol Donachy

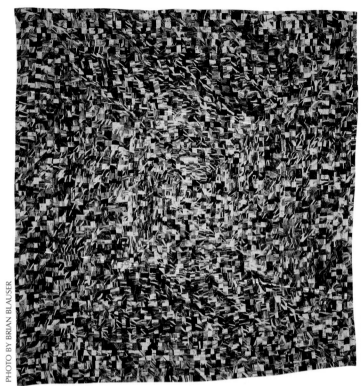

***Cranesbill,***
37½" x 41½",
student quilt
by Doris Koozer
(radiating composition)

***Red Eye,***
74" x 76",
by Phil D. Jones
(circular composition)

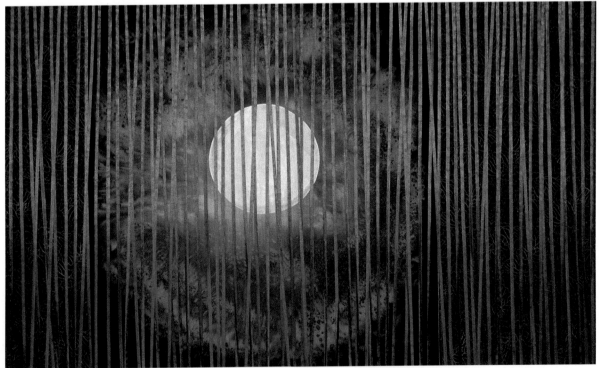

***Through the Trees: Solstice Moon,*** 68" x 39", by Chris Wolf Edmonds (vertical composition)

# Analogous
# Color Scheme

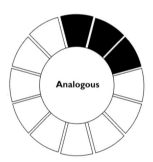

$A$nalogous colors are next to each other on the color wheel. They work well with each other because they are closely related and share a primary color.

**Analogous**

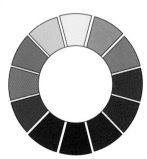

## EXERCISE 1: ZOOMING IN

Zoom in to create a dynamic, nature-inspired composition with an analogous color scheme.

### ■ Materials

- Fused fabric in an analogous color scheme (for example, red, red-orange, and orange **or** blue, blue-green, and green), including the tints and shades, in solid or print fabrics
- White fabric: 1 piece 8$^1/_2$" x 11" for background foundation
- Picture of a plant or flower
- Pencil
- Copy paper
- Tracing paper
- Iron
- Copier

### ■ Directions

**1.** If your picture is smaller than 2", enlarge it to at least 3 times its size (300%). Move the viewfinder (created on page 36) around the picture until you see an exciting design that conforms to one of the compositions in *The Nine-Patch of Compositions.* Tape down the viewfinder. Trace the design onto tracing paper to create a contour line drawing within the rectangle.

**Picture and enlargement**

**Viewfinder in place**

**2.** Enlarge your tracing paper line drawing by 400% to 8¹/₂" x 11". Make 2 copies of the line drawing for templates. Trace your design onto a piece of white 8¹/₂" x 11" fabric. (If you prefer to fuse to paper, make an extra copy of your drawing.)

**Tracing paper contour drawing**

**Enlarged line drawing**

**3.** You need a black-and-white copy of your picture for a value comparison. Make a black-and-white copy or take a black-and-white photo of the picture. If you are using a digital image, you can convert the color digital image to black and white using photo-editing software.

**4.** Match the values of your colored fabrics to the gray-scale values on the black-and-white copy or photo to make sure you use a full seven-step value run (see page 35).

**5. Cut** out the templates, **flip** them over, and **trace** around them on the paper backing of the fused fabrics. Cut the fabric on the drawn lines, remove the backing, and fuse the shapes in **place** on the foundation.

## The Why Box

*Zooming in brings the viewer closer to the subject matter and eliminates unnecessary distractions. Analogous color schemes are harmonious and serene because the colors are closely related.*

**Diagonal composition**
by Katie Pasquini Masopust

**Diagonal composition**
by Linda Pysto

**Asymmetrical composition**
by Doris Koozer

**Radiating composition**
by Christi Low

**Asymmetrical composition**
by Venisa M. Gallegos

# ■ ANALOGOUS COLOR QUILTS

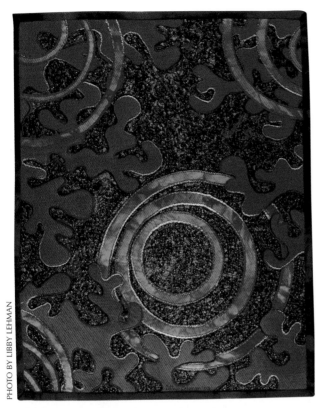

PHOTO BY LIBBY LEHMAN

***Ripple I,*** 11" x 14", by Libby Lehman (circular composition)

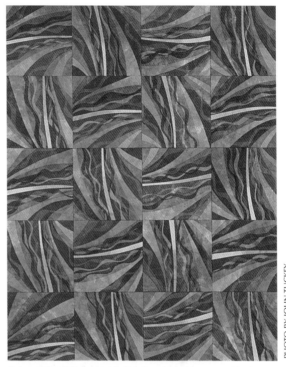

PHOTO BY JOHN TUCKEY

***Salsa,*** 42" x 52", by Nelda Warkentin (grid composition)

PHOTO BY HAWTHORNE STUDIO

***Buddha III,*** 30" x 45", acrylic painting on wood
by Brett Barker (grid composition)

PHOTO BY BOB ADAMS

***Rectangular Image No. 3,*** 52" x 40",
by Bob Adams (horizontal composition)

***Flowers,***
19" x 22",
student-painted fabric
by Christi Low
(diagonal composition)

# Warm or Cool
## Color Scheme

Warm colors—red, orange, and yellow—are seen in fire; cool colors—blue, green, and violet—are seen in water. Warm color schemes create quilts that are vibrant and exciting. Cool color schemes create quilts that are tranquil and soothing. Warm colors advance and cool colors recede, so you can create innovative landscapes by combining these color schemes.

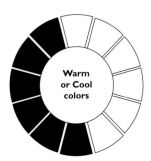

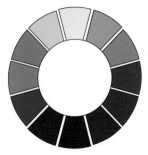

## EXERCISE 1: LANDSCAPE

Divide the color wheel in half so that warm colors are on one side and cool colors on the other. You will be creating landscapes with these different temperatures.

### ■ Materials

- Fused fabrics in either warm **or** cool colors, including the tints and shades—for example, warm colors of red-violet, red, red-orange, orange, yellow-orange, and yellow **or** cool colors of violet, blue-violet, blue, blue-green, green, and yellow-green. (Use your color wheel and gray scale for reference.)
- White fabric: 1 piece 8½" x 11" for background foundation
- Picture of a landscape
- Copy paper
- Iron
- Pencil
- Tracing paper

### ■ Directions

1. Place tracing paper over the picture, and trace the landscape, simplifying the shapes (see page 10 on simplifying).

**Drawing with tracing paper**

**Landscape picture and simplified drawing**

**2.** Analyze the drawing according to *The Nine-Patch of Compositions.* Redraw the design, moving elements as necessary. Make 1 copy for the templates. Trace your design onto a piece of white 8½" x 11" fabric. (If you prefer to fuse to paper, make an extra copy of your design.)

**3.** Follow the values in the landscape. **Cut** out the shapes from the template copy, **flip** them over, and **trace** them onto the paper backing of the fused fabric of either your warm or cool colors. Remove the backing, and fuse the shapes in **place.** Save the templates for the optional exercises that follow.

**Vertical composition, medium-value warm colors** by Katie Pasquini Masopust

### ■ Optional Exercise

Repeat the process with fabrics of the opposite temperature.

**Vertical composition, medium-value cool colors** by Katie Pasquini Masopust

### ■ Optional Exercise

Repeat the process with warm and cool fabrics together, using one as the dominant element and the other as accent. Warm colors advance and cool recede. If warm colors predominate, use the cool accent where it will accentuate the most depth. If the cool colors predominate, use a warm accent so that the closest elements pop out.

## The Why Box

*Because warm colors advance, you can use them to create close-up views of landscapes. Because cool colors recede, you can use them to create panoramic landscapes. When using both color temperatures, warm is placed in the foreground and cool in the distance—this uses the temperatures of colors to enhance the depth of the drawing.*

*Any landscape design can be made stronger by altering it to conform to one of the compositions of* The Nine-Patch of Compositions.

**Dominant warm colors with accents of cool (including tints and shades), diagonal composition** by Brett Barker

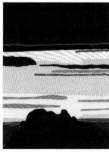

**Warm colors, horizontal composition** by Linda Sue Minette

**Warm colors, horizontal composition** by Jo Anne Valentine Powell

**Cool colors, framed composition** by Marie Longserre

**Cool colors, diagonal composition** by Linda Eslinger

PHOTO BY HAWTHORNE STUDIO

***Canyon,*** 96" x 54",
by Katie Pasquini Masopust
(framed composition)

PHOTO BY JOAN COLVIN

***Raw Heat,*** 19" x 24", student quilt
by Dawn Siden (asymmetrical composition)

***Madrone #11,*** 29" x 56¹/₂",
by Joan Colvin (diagonal composition)

## ◼ COOL-COLOR QUILTS

***Orchard II,*** 26" x 16",
painting on board by Brett
Barker (diagonal composition)

***Birch Trees,*** 18" x 18", by Ree Nancarrow
(asymmetrical composition)

## ◼ COMBINATION OF WARM AND COOL

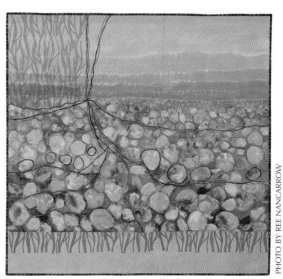

***River Bar With Willows,***
42" x 40", by Ree Nancarrow
(horizontal composition)

***Frogzilla,*** 32¹/₂" x 44¹/₂",
by Wendy Hill (framed composition)

# Complementary
# Color Scheme

Complementary colors are opposite each other on the color wheel. These colors vibrate when placed next to each other, often to the extent that the viewer's eyes cannot focus. The following exercises will show you how to use complementary color schemes effectively.

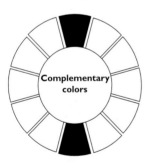

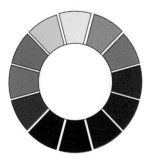

## EXERCISE 1: LINEAR DESIGN WITH STRIPS

Fabric strips will be used to create complementary compositions.

### ■ Materials
- Fused fabrics in a pair of value 4 complementary colors (red/green, blue/orange, **or** yellow/violet), including a tint and a shade for each selected color (Use your color wheel and gray scale for reference.)
- White fabric: 3 pieces 8½" x 11" for background foundations
- Rotary cutting ruler
- Rotary cutter
- Cutting mat
- Iron

### ■ Directions
**1.** Remove the paper backing from the value 4 fabrics, and use a rotary cutter and ruler to cut strips of varying widths of the true-value complementary colors. (Don't use the tints and shades at this point.) Use the ruler **only** as a straightedge; don't measure the widths of your strips—cut varying widths freehand.

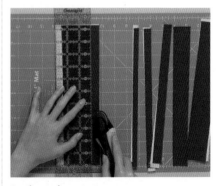

**Cutting strips**

**2.** Use the strips to create an 8½" x 11" composition from *The Nine-Patch of Compositions.* Anything goes, as long as only straight strips are used; they may be cut in any way you like. Fill the entire sheet, leaving no white showing. You will have strips left over that you will use in the next step and exercise.

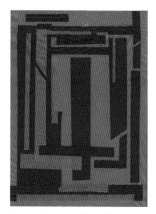

**Framed composition** by Brett Barker

**3.** Cut strips of the light (the tint) and the dark (the shade) of both complementary colors. Combine them with the leftover strips from your first piece, building on the same composition from *The Nine-Patch of Compositions*. Create a second piece that is mainly 1 color, with accents of its complement. For example, if you are using orange and blue, create a piece that is primarily orange with accents of blue. Aim for 80% orange and 20% blue. Again, anything goes, as long as you cover the entire piece (leave no white showing).

**Framed composition with tints and shades** by Brett Barker

## ■ Optional Exercise

Create a third piece that is the reverse of the color scheme created in Step 3. For example, when you use orange and blue, the third piece will be 80% blue with 20% orange accents. No white!

*The Why Box*

Medium value (value 4) complementary colors cause eye vibration. That is great when you are trying to initially catch someone's attention (it is often used in advertising), but this color scheme can be very tiring to the eye. With the addition of more values through the use of the tints and shades, the vibration is decreased, creating a more palatable, yet still exciting, piece.

*Bow Tie Sunset,*
40" x 31", student quilt
by Barbara J. LaLiberte
(blue/orange complementary
framed composition)

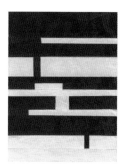

**Horizontal composition**
by Katie Pasquini Masopust

**Horizontal composition
with tints and shades**
by Katie Pasquini Masopust

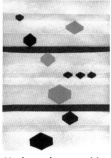

**Horizontal composition
with tints and shades**
by Katie Pasquini Masopust

PHOTO BY JAN C. WATTEN

**Burbank Strip Quilt**
59" x 59",
by Ellen Oppenheimer
(red/green complementary
grid composition)

PHOTO BY CAROL SHINN

**Red Truck, Green Truck,**
20" x 25¹/₂",
by Carol Shinn
(red/green complementary
diagonal composition)

**Vertical composition**
by Sharon Signorelli

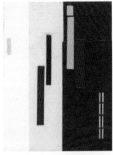

**Vertical composition with tints
and shades** by Sharon Signorelli

**Vertical composition**
by Rebecca Chapin

**Diagonal composition with tints
and shades** by Rebecca Chapin

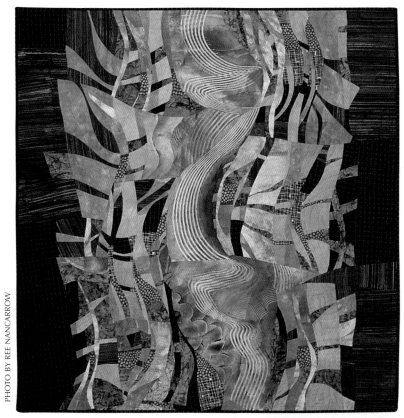

**Spring Run-Off II**
52" x 53¹/₂",
by Ree Nancarrow (purple/yellow
complementary vertical composition)

PHOTO BY REE NANCARROW

**Gardener's Milagro,**
20" x 23",
by Jane Burch Cochran
(red/green complementary
framed composition)

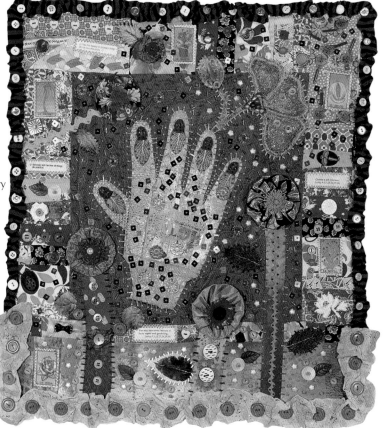

PHOTO BY PAMELA BRAUN

# Split AND Dual Complementary Color Schemes

As you saw in the previous chapter, complementary color schemes are very vibrant. Split and dual complementary color schemes can be very energetic without the jarring quality of a straight complement.

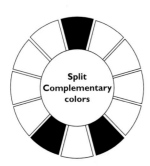

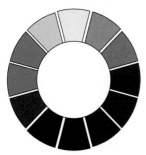

## EXERCISE 1: SPLIT COMPLEMENTARY ARCHITECTURAL DESIGN

Architectural forms are fun to cut in a free-form fashion. There are many types of inspiration; architecture is just one of them. Feel free to use any subject matter that inspires you.

For the first exercise, use a split complementary color scheme. Put your finger on any color on your wheel. Draw an imaginary line straight across your wheel until you reach the complement. On either side of this complement, you'll see the two colors needed to create a split complementary color scheme. You're literally "splitting" the complement to get this new three-color scheme.

### ■ Materials
- Fused fabrics in split complementary colors, including the tints and shades (Use your color wheel for reference.)
- White fabric: 1 piece 8½" x 11" for background foundation
- Picture with an architectural theme
- Rotary cutting ruler
- Rotary cutter
- Cutting mat
- Iron
- Timer

### ■ Directions
1. Analyze your picture to see how it conforms to any of the compositions in *The Nine-Patch of Compositions*. You will need to emphasize a particular composition as you complete the next steps.

**2.** Remove the paper backing from the fused fabrics. Set your timer for 30 minutes. Free-cut the fabric in relation to the shapes and images in the picture, simplifying as you go (refer to the contour cutting exercises on pages 20–22) —no templates, no measurements. Place your fabrics on the foundation, moving or adding elements if you need to emphasize your compositional choice. This should be fast, free, and fun! Fuse the shapes in place.

PHOTO BY KATIE PASQUNI MASOPUST

**Adobe building**

**Free-cutting fabric**

## ■ SPLIT COMPLEMENTARY QUILTS

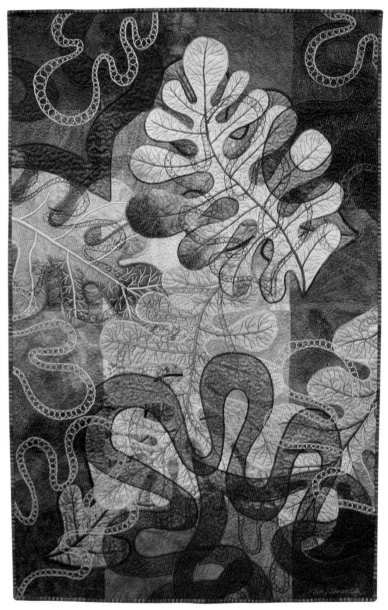

PHOTO BY LIBBY LEHMAN

***Drift III,*** 31" x 47", by Libby Lehman
(purple/yellow-green/yellow-orange split complementary grid composition)

**Diagonal composition**
by Christi Low

**Horizontal composition**
by Deb Martin

**Vertical composition**
by Ann Malone

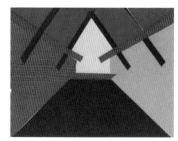

**Symmetrical composition**
by Vinda Robison

PHOTO BY ROBERT COMINGSS

**Trees in the City,**
26" x 26",
by Linda MacDonald
(blue/yellow-orange/
red-orange split
complementary
vertical composition)

## The Why Box

*Value 4 complementary color schemes are jarring, as we noted in the previous chapter. Using the two colors on either side of the complement lessens the vibration because they are once removed from the stronger complement. These color schemes are dynamic without being overpowering.*

*Eliminating the use of templates and putting the piece together in a fast, free way allows your right-brained creativity to flow.*

# EXERCISE 2: DUAL COMPLEMENTARY ARCHITECTURAL DESIGN

For this exercise, use a dual complementary color scheme: Put your fingers on two colors next to each other on the wheel; with both fingers draw imaginary lines **straight across** your wheel until you reach the two complements. These four colors make up a dual complementary color scheme.

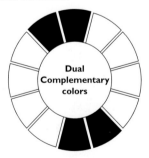

Dual
Complementary
colors

## ■ Materials

- Same architectural picture used in the previous exercise
- Fused fabrics in dual complementary colors (for example, violet and red-violet, yellow and yellow-green) and the tints and shades (Use your color wheel and gray scale for reference.)
- White fabric: 1 piece 8¹/₂" x 11" for background foundation
- Pencil
- Copy paper
- Rotary cutting ruler
- Rotary cutter
- Cutting mat
- Iron

## ■ Directions

1. Draw 4 large rectangles on a piece of 8¹/₂" x 11" paper, filling the page. It is not necessary to use a ruler; these rectangles are frames for your drawings.

**Four rectangles on a page**

**Picture**

**2.** In the first frame, simplify your architectural picture—alter each shape by drawing it as either a square or rectangle. In the next frame, draw the picture again, using only ovals or circles. In the third frame, draw the picture using only triangles.

**3.** Fill in the final frame using a combination of the shapes from the first 3 drawings.

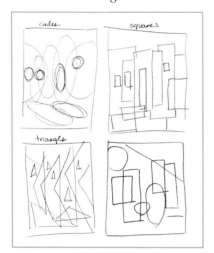

**Series of simplified drawings**

**Steps 2 & 3**

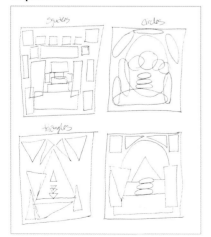

**Simplified drawings**
by Linda Eslinger

**4.** Set aside the inspiration picture. Choose your favorite of the 4 drawings. Enlarge it by redrawing on 8¹/₂" x 11" paper, making it conform to a composition from *The Nine-Patch of Compositions.* Draw the image twice more, enhancing each drawing as you build on the original, so you have a total of 3 large drawings.

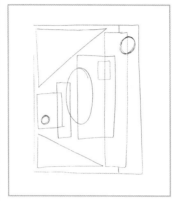

**Enlarged, improved, favorite drawing**

**5.** Choose 1 of the 3 drawings. If you like to use templates, make a copy of this drawing for the

**Step 4**

**Enlarged, improved drawing**
by Linda Eslinger

templates. Trace your drawing onto a piece of white 8¹/₂" x 11" fabric. (If you prefer to fuse to paper, make an extra copy of your drawing.) **Cut** out the shapes from the template copy, **flip** them over, **trace** onto the paper backing of the fused fabric, and fuse the shapes in **place**. Use the tints for the lightest areas and the shades for the darkest areas. If you prefer to free-cut, look at your drawing for reference as you free-cut colors and shapes, then place them onto your fabric.

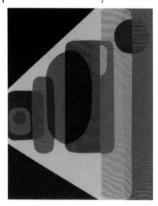

*The Why Box*

*An effective way to build an exciting color scheme that retains some vibration, without actually tiring the eye, is to use the full value ranges of dual complementary colors. By changing the architectural image to simple shapes, you learn to compose more abstractly. Making a sequence of drawings is a great way to improve your compositional skills.*

**Framed composition**
by Linda Eslinger

# ■ DUAL COMPLEMENTARY QUILTS

PHOTO BY JOHN G. LANNING

***Marsh 14,*** 52" x 16³/₄", by Sue Benner (blue/orange blue-green/red-orange dual complementary horizontal composition)

PHOTO BY JAY YORK

PHOTO BY JAY YORK

***Tree of Knowledge,*** 26" x 37", student quilt by Linda Eslinger (framed composition)

***Many Winters,*** 82" x 68", by Jo Diggs (blue/orange blue-violet/orange dual complementary symmetrical composition)

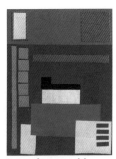

**Framed composition**
by Deb Martin

**Vertical composition**
by Ann Malone

**Symmetrical composition**
by Vinda Robison

**Framed composition**
by Linda Eslinger

**Vertical composition**
by Christi Low

# Triadic
# Color Scheme

A triadic color scheme uses three colors that are equidistant from each other on the wheel, creating an equilateral triangle.

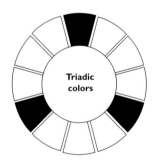

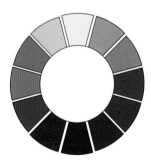

## EXERCISE 1: NONREPRESENTATIONAL DESIGN

In an abstract composition, something real is made to look less real. (See abstract contour cutting exercise on page 22.) In contrast, a nonrepresentational composition is created solely from your imagination without any realistic inspirations.

### ■ Materials

- Fused fabrics in triadic colors– for example, yellow-orange, red violet, and blue-green, or the primaries: red, yellow, and blue, and the tints and shades (Use your color wheel and gray scale for reference.)
- White fabric: 1 piece 8½" x 11" for background foundation
- Pencil
- Copy paper
- Rotary cutting ruler
- Rotary cutter
- Cutting mat
- Iron

### ■ Directions

**1.** Draw a frame around the edges of your paper without using a ruler.

**2.** Create a nonrepresentational drawing using 6–7 geometric shapes (squares, circles, rectangles, triangles, and so on). Some of the shapes can go off the edge of your frame. Think about scale as you draw, making some shapes large and some small.

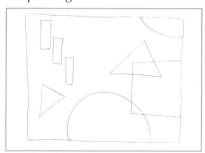

**Drawing with shapes**

**3.** Make a second drawing, building on the first by using a **dominant shape**. The dominant shape is used **more** than all the others. This is a numbers game—it doesn't matter how big or small your shapes are—it is the **number** of shapes that determines dominance. All other shapes, the secondary shapes, should accentuate, or play off, the dominant shape.

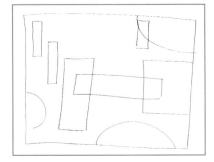

Drawing adjusted to have a dominant shape (rectangle)

**4. Count** the number of shapes to make sure that 1 shape is dominant. If 1 shape doesn't dominate, try again, adding shapes. For example, if you have 5 dominant squares, 4 triangles, and 3 rectangles, your spread isn't large enough—you need many more squares in relation to the other shapes. A better spread would be 10 squares, 3 triangles, and 2 rectangles.

**5.** Look at the drawing to see whether there is a composition emerging according to *The Nine-Patch of Compositions*. If you have a composition with a dominant shape, enhance it—if not, create another drawing.

Don't think too much as you create these drawings—go for what is spontaneous and intuitive. Sometimes you just have to "do it" and see where the composition takes you. Look at your drawings, and choose your favorite.

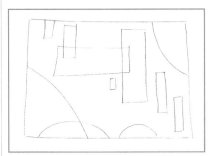

Drawing improved to conform to the composition chosen (diagonal)

**6.** Notice shapes that might naturally overlap other shapes; erase some lines so you have an overlapping design with depth.

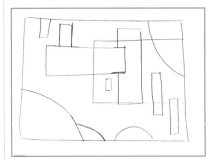

Erase some lines for more depth.

**7.** Use a piece of copy paper to cover an edge of your drawing. Move the paper inward from the frame, covering the side of your drawing as you go. Stop when you intuitively feel that your drawing looks better, and tape the blank sheet of paper over your drawing.

Crop with a blank page.

**8.** If necessary, use 3 more sheets of paper, and repeat this process from all sides until you find a pleasing design that conforms to a composition in *The Nine-Patch of Compositions*. If you need to emphasize your compositional choice, add more lines or shapes. You may not need to cover all 4 sides of your drawing to find a composition that you like; go for what is quick and intuitive. Tape down all the blank sheets of paper. You have now cropped your design.

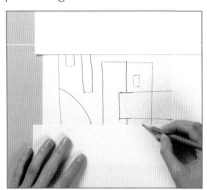

Cropping pages taped down

**9.** Enlarge your drawing by hand, following to the steps for contour drawing (see pages 16–18), adding lines if necessary.

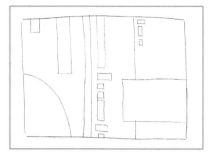

**Lines added to enhance the composition to a vertical composition after cropping**

**10.** Make a copy of the enlarged drawing for the templates. Trace your design onto a piece of white 8¹/₂" x 11" fabric. (If you prefer to fuse to paper, make an extra copy of your enlarged drawing.)

**11.** Create depth by advancing the lighter colors (putting them in front) and receding the darker colors (placing them in back). To do this, **cut** out the shapes for the foreground from your template copy. Pick your lightest fabrics (values 1, 2, and 3), **flip** the template shapes over, **trace** around them, and fuse the shapes in **place**.

**12.** Work from the front to the back. **Flip, trace, cut,** and **place** your triadic fabrics to fill the composition. Be sure your darkest fabrics (values 6 and 7) are placed in the background—you may have to arbitrarily assign a background to your piece. Don't leave any white space!

### The Why Box

*It is very important to create more than one drawing before undertaking a project. Dominant shapes help create a more cohesive design. A triadic color scheme can be challenging because the three colors are so widely separated on the color wheel, but with tints in the front and shades toward the back, the illusion of depth can create an exciting piece.*

### ■ TRIADIC COLOR QUILTS

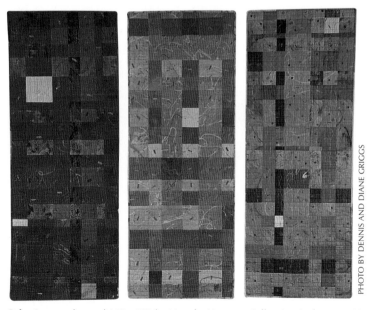

PHOTO BY DENNIS AND DIANE GRIGGS

*Color Jazz,* each panel 23" x 58", by Natasha Kempers-Cullen (vertical composition)

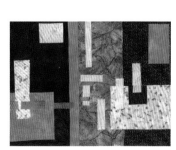

**Vertical composition**
by Brett Barker

**Framed composition**
by Venisa M. Gallegos

**Horizontal composition**
by Barbara LaLiberte

**Vertical composition**
by Sue Kongs

PHOTO BY SABILA SAVAGE

***Reflections 5: Sunset on the Nile,***
65" x 51",
by Jean Neblett
(diagonal composition)

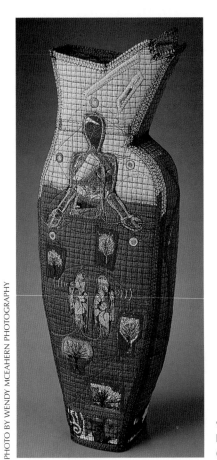

PHOTO BY WENDY MCEAHERN PHOTOGRAPHY

***Wilderness,***
9" x 26" x 5",
by Kay Khan
(vertical composition)

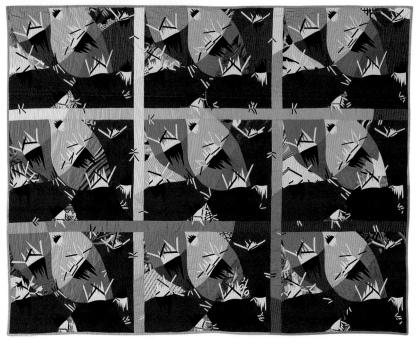

PHOTO BY DAVID BELDA

***Primal I,***
75" x 58",
by Jean Neblett
(grid composition)

# Rainbow
# Color Scheme

A rainbow color scheme uses all the colors in the color wheel. Some medium-value colors (the pure hues) are naturally lighter and some are naturally darker (for example, yellow is the lightest pure hue, at 12 o'clock on the color wheel, and violet is the darkest, at 6 o'clock).

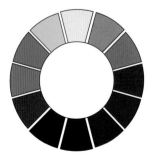

## EXERCISE 1: ARCHITECTURAL DESIGN

One way to play with the rainbow of colors is to escape from reality and use them strictly to create depth. In this exercise, you'll use architectural forms as inspiration because the architectural elements allow you to understand the natural values of the color wheel.

### ▦ Materials

- Fused fabrics of all 12 of the medium-value, true-hue colors of the color wheel (Use the colors in the middle of your color wheel, no tints or shades.)
- White fabric: 1 piece 8½" x 11" for background foundation
- Architectural picture
- Pencil
- Copy paper
- Tracing paper
- Rotary cutting ruler
- Rotary cutter
- Cutting mat
- Iron

### ▦ Directions

1. Choose a picture or make a simple drawing from your imagination of an architectural structure or architectural element.

**2.** Create a simplified drawing from your picture. Enlarge it as you redraw, making sure it conforms to a composition in *The Nine-Patch of Compositions.*

**Rancho de Taos**

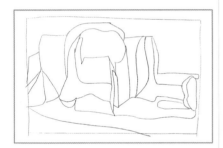

**Simplified drawing**

**3.** Make a copy of the drawing for the templates. Trace your drawing onto a piece of white 8¹/₂" x 11" fabric. (If you prefer to fuse to paper, make an extra copy of your drawing.)

**4.** Lay your colors out in order, from light to dark. You will notice that yellow-green and magenta (red-violet) are sometimes difficult to fit in because they contain equal amounts of warm and cool, so they appear to advance and recede differently from what is logical. Let your intuition and composition guide you when using these 2 colors.

**Light to dark: yellow in front and violet in back**

**5.** Analyze your drawing, and determine which shapes are farthest from you. Use violet for those shapes. **Cut** out the shapes from the template copy. **Flip** them over, and **trace** them onto the back of the fused fabrics. Fuse the shapes in **place**.

**6.** Work your way forward. **Cut, flip, trace,** and fuse your pieces in **place**. Be sure to use violet for your background; go through all 12 colors as you move forward, until the foreground is created with yellow. This will create depth through placement of color. Use yellow-green and magenta (red-violet) as accents.

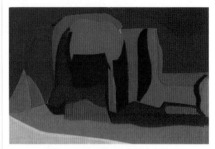

**Asymmetrical composition** by Katie Pasquini Masopust

## The Why Box

*By creating an architectural piece in the rainbow color scheme, you will get a better sense of what colors naturally appear to come forward in a piece and which appear to recede. Using a simplified abstraction makes it easier to understand and use the inherent value depth of each color.*

### ■ RAINBOW COLOR QUILTS

***Pueblo,*** 45" x 25", by Katie Pasquini Masopust (horizontal composition)

# ■ RAINBOW COLOR QUILTS

*Artfabrik,*
51" x 51",
by Laura Wasilowski
(circular composition)

PHOTO BY LAURA WASILOWSKI

PHOTO BY MICHAEL JAMES

*Square Dance Interweave,*
50" x 50",
by Michael James
(grid composition)

PHOTO BY PAMELA BRAUN

*3 Madison Lane, Nutcrackers,*
60" x 63",
by Terrie Hancock Mangat
(framed composition)

PHOTO BY HAWTHORNE STUDIO

*Glass Crystals,*
86" x 45",
by Katie Pasquini Masopust
(horizontal composition)

# Expanding
# Your Knowledge

In this chapter, we'll show you ways to expand on your newly-found artistic knowledge by considering transparency, colors from nature, and geometric focal points. It's best to get comfortable with the principles in the preceding chapters before you add these concepts to your repertoire.

## EXERCISE 1: TRANSPARENCY

Transparency is the effect of being able to see through to another layer, as if two pieces of colored cellophane are overlapped, creating a third color as they cross. Instead of using sheer fabric to create transparencies, you will create the effect with opaque fabrics. When mixing paints, equal amounts of red and yellow create orange. As a textile artist, you can visually mix these colors by using the techniques in this exercise.

### ■ Materials
- Fused fabric in all the colors from the color wheel, including the tints and shades
- Gray fabric: 1 piece 8½" x 11" for background
- Pencil
- Rotary cutting ruler
- Rotary cutter
- Cutting mat
- Scissors
- Iron

### ■ Directions

**1.** Cut several 2" x 2" squares of each color. Remove the paper backing from the fabrics as you cut them.

**2.** Lay a square of red and a square of yellow so that they overlap in the middle of the gray fabric. Touch the tip of the iron to each of the squares to hold them in place.

**3.** Use a pencil to draw the edge of the piece hidden underneath the top square. **Cut** out this overlap shape, and use it as a template to cut the transparency color—orange. **Flip** the little template over onto the back of an orange square, mark, and cut out. Remove the paper backing from the fabric.

**4.** Place the orange piece in the proper position so its edges complete the edges of both the original squares, creating the look of 2 squares overlapping. Fuse the orange piece in place.

**Red and yellow create orange.**

**5.** Lay a blue square over a portion of the yellow square. The place where they overlap will create a transparency of green. Use the same process as above and draw the overlap, cut it away, and use it for a template to cut the green. Place the green in the proper spot, making sure that it completes each square.

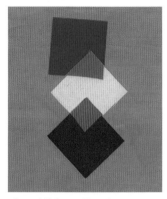

**Blue added to yellow for green transparency.**

**6.** Lay a blue square over a portion of the red square to create a transparency of violet. You have now used all the primary colors—red, yellow, and blue—to create the secondary colors of orange, green, and violet.

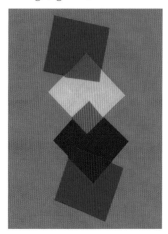

**Blue added to red for violet transparency.**

**7.** Use this same process to create the tertiary colors.

**Combining to create the tertiary colors: orange and yellow to create yellow-orange, red and orange to create red-orange, violet and red to create red-violet, blue and violet to create blue-violet, green and blue to create blue-green**

**8.** Add white to create the tints. The difference in value also creates the effect of a transparency.

**White added to several colors**

**9.** Add black to these colors to create the shades. Differences in value create the transparency.

**Black added to several colors**

Be sure that the overlays create a continuous line to represent the perfect square.

**Incorrect placement of transparency square**   **Correct placement of transparency square**

*The Why Box*

*This exercise demonstrates the use of the color wheel for visually mixing fabrics to create transparency. By adding transparencies to your quilts, you give them a light, multilayered, airy feeling.*

PHOTO BY ERIC KIEVIT

*Joris Lutz,*
52" x 72",
by Leslie Gabrielse
(diagonal composition)

PHOTO BY HAWTHORNE STUDIO

*Ice Cave,*
54" x 90",
by Katie Pasquini Masopust
(vertical composition)

PHOTO BY HAWTHORNE STUDIO

*Sunny Side Up,*
44" x 44",
by Katie Pasquini Masopust
(horizontal composition)

# EXERCISE 2: COLORS FROM NATURE

There are many color schemes beyond *The Nine-Patch of Color Schemes*. Mother Nature is a true colorist, providing inspiration through the color combinations of the flora and fauna around us. In this exercise, you will create a series of 3" x 5" cards that capture these color schemes.

### ◼ Materials

- Pictures of a flower and an animal
- Magazine ad (optional)
- Fused fabrics in the colors of the flower and animal
- 3" x 5" index card
- Rotary cutting ruler
- Rotary cutter
- Cutting mat
- Iron

### ◼ Directions

**1.** Look closely at the picture of the flower. Be sure to notice all the subtle differences in the colors. Work with proportion by filling the 3" x 5" card with the same proportion of color as is found in the flower. Pick the most prominent color, and cut a strip of that color in the amount that you see in the picture. If it is a red flower and about 40% of the picture is red, cut a strip that covers 40% of the 3" x 5" card (use your eye to discern the proportions rather than measuring). If the yellow center is about 5% of the picture, cut a yellow strip that covers 5% of the card, and so on.

**Flower and its proportional colors**

**Flower and its proportional colors**

**2.** Use all the colors and their subtle value changes. Continue until the entire card is covered proportionally and you have used all the colors in the flower.

**3.** Fuse the strips to the 3" x 5" card.

**4.** Repeat the process, using a picture of an animal. Look closely for all the different colors. Approximate the percentage of each color, and cover that percentage of the 3" x 5" card for each.

**Koala and its proportional colors**

**Frog and its proportional colors**

ALL PHOTOS ON THIS PAGE
BY KATIE PASQUINI MASOPUST

### ◼ Optional Exercise

Repeat the process of the exercise above, this time using a magazine ad that caught your eye because of the color. It is always fun to see how advertising designers use color.

## The Why 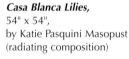Box

Subtle color changes and varying proportions make a more interesting color scheme. The 3" x 5" cards make a great reference tool. Save these cards in a card file box and pull them out when you start a quilt to find ideas for your color schemes. Whenever you feel stuck for ideas, reach for a picture and do this fun exercise.

*Casa Blanca Lilies,*
54" x 54",
by Katie Pasquini Masopust
(radiating composition)

*River,* 10" x 10",
by Darcy Falk
(diagonal composition)

**Tesuque Aspen**, 19" x 25", pastel painting by
Brett Barker (vertical composition)

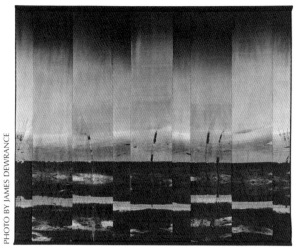

**North Light,**
68" x 56",
by Judith Content
(grid composition)

**Sun Kissed,**
168" x 65",
by Velda Newman
(horizontal composition)

**Melon Study,**
36" x 20",
by Velda Newman
(circular composition)

# EXERCISE 3: GET YOUR FOCAL POINT IN SHAPE

You can change the shape or design of a focal point to render it even more eye-catching. For this exercise, use whatever color scheme and compositional arrangement you enjoy.

## ■ Materials

- Fused fabrics in a seven-step value run of 1 color (if you want a monochromatic design) or more colors (if you prefer)
- White fabric: 1 piece 8½" x 11" for background foundation
- Copy paper
- Iron

## ■ Directions

**1.** Follow Steps 1–4 on pages 35–36.

**2.** Locate the focal point on the enlarged copy or on your white fabric foundation. Pick a simple geometric shape: a circle, square, rectangle, or triangle. Use a pencil to draw this shape around the focal point. Cut out this shape.

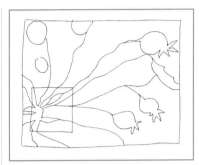
**Drawing with focal point**

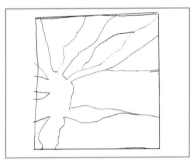
**Cut out square focal point.**

**3.** Cut out the shapes within your geometric focal point.

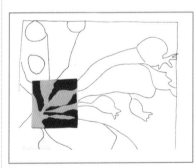
**Geometric focal point**

**4.** Choose value step fabrics 1 and 7, just as you did on page 35, to create a dynamic focal point.

**5.** Follow the instructions for Steps 5–6 on page 36 to complete your piece.

## ■ GEOMETRIC FOCAL POINT QUILT

***Glen Eyrie Berries,***
26" x 33", student quilt by Vinda Robison (radiating composition)

*The Why Box*

*You now have a design that, while conforming to a composition in* The Nine-Patch of Compositions, *also has a geometric focal point, attracting your eye. A geometrically shaped focal point can be used to either reinforce or alter your design choice.*

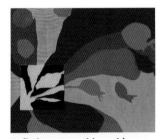
**Radiating composition with square focal point** by Vinda Robison

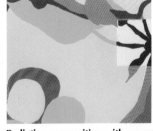
**Radiating composition with square focal point** by Doris Koozer

**Diagonal composition with circular focal points** by Christi Low

# I Did Everything Right! But...

Sometimes even established artists have pieces that, to them, are less than successful. You learn from your failures as well as from your successes.

The following brave, established artists have agreed to show some of their failures and to explain how they learned from them, so that you too can learn. As you look at the following quilts, think about how **you** would fix the following problems if they occurred in your projects.

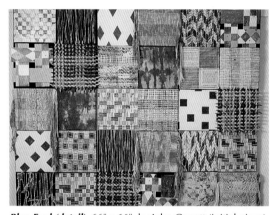

***Blue Fool (detail),*** 66" x 66", by John Garrett (initial piece)

John Garrett says he was "interested in juxtaposing different patterns created in different ways using different materials. The result, *Blue Fool,* was a flop." In subsequent pieces, "I changed the size of the individual squares. I did another blue-and-white quilt called *The Ensign's Confession,* and it works much better than *Blue Fool.*"

***The Ensign's Confession,*** 75" x 75", by John Garrett (improved piece)

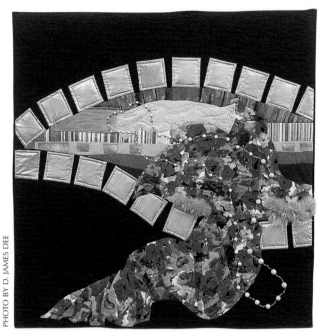

**Overload,** 55¹/₂" x 55¹/₂", by Randy Frost
(initial piece)

"I bought just the right fabric," says Randy Frost, auditioned a dozen other fabrics to get a perfect metallic look, and stitched folds into printed fabric with great care—all to no avail. When *Overload* was hung on my studio wall, one look told me it was a disaster. I, too, was on overload with unrealistic expectations for this quilt.

"Artist friends offered suggestions, but only one idea made sense—a chain saw. Stopping one step short of that radical act, I made a more positive decision—end the series and see what happens. In fact, something was already happening. Using half of the visual concept of the zipper, I realized I was making pathways." *Markers* is an example of that new work.

**Markers,**
10" x 11¹/₂",
by Randy Frost
(improved piece)

Judith Trager says, "In the first version of *Watermelon Summer,* the colors, although complementary, don't play against each other to make a unified piece. The color is good, but nothing glows."

Judith "corrected the quilt by adding an extra layer of appliquéd leaves and heavily stitching into the leaves, creating another layer. This makes the heavy complementary colors sing."

**Watermelon Summer,**
51" x 54",
by Judith Trager
(initial piece)

**Watermelon Summer,**
51" x 54",
by Judith Trager
(improved piece)

**The Piper Stones III,**
58" x 26",
by Denise Labadie
(initial piece)

**Stones of Kilclooney Moor,** 28" x 18", by Denise Labadie (improved piece)

When discussing *The Piper Stones III,* Denise Labadie says, "I was trying to work with shadows in a different way than I had with other landscapes. I didn't plan it out correctly. It is confusing to look at and is not believable. I enrolled in a class on light and shadow, and it taught me to look at light a different way. *Stones of Kilclooney Moor* was the next quilt I made after the class."

Nancy Erickson says that in *Interiors #2*, "The woman is out of shape, and it matters that she is out of shape. I tried and tried to get it right, and even entered it in a show where it appeared, to my embarrassment, on the flyer! By this time I'd decided to shelve it. A failure. One feels so impatient when this happens, so I quickly went on with the next piece, *Interiors #3*, which worked better right away."

**Interiors #2,** 56" x 80", by Nancy Erickson (initial piece)

**Interiors #3,** 54" x 90", by Nancy Erickson (improved piece)

"I had a piece of horse fabric that I loved," says Chris Wolf Edmonds, "so I pieced strips in a manner I had used successfully in the past. When the top was completed, it definitely didn't work. Why I hung it up on the barn wall and took a picture of it, I will never know…and a detail! A year later I pulled it out and attacked it with paint. I didn't start over to create a new piece, I just painted over the original. I still wouldn't list it as one of my best works, but it was greatly improved, and *Inside/Outside* found a buyer who liked it."

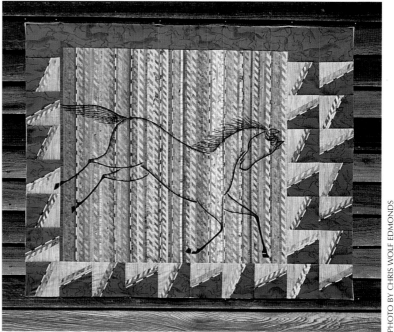

*Inside/Outside,* 50" x 40", by Chris Wolf Edmonds (initial piece)

*Inside/Outside,* 50" x 40, by Chris Wolf Edmonds (improved piece)

In *Big Sticks,* I wanted to take a photo of an old rotting pile of sticks and make it into something beautiful with color. I chose complementary colors for the individual sticks. The light side would be the warm color with its complement for the shadows. I added black and white and gray to give a bit of relief from the jarring complements. The whole piece is much too chaotic for me.

I realized that the reason for the chaos was that the complementary colors were all medium values with no tints or shades, and the one-on-one color matching was too harsh. I chose a different subject in *Big Sticks* and used a variety of values of the complementary colors within the individual leaves.

To quiet the chaos, I used the three full leaves to create a radiating composition in yellow and purple. The remaining leaves use the complements of red and green, and orange and blue. The background is chaotic, but the yellow and purple leaves hold everything in place, creating order.

*Big Sticks,*
70" x 60",
by Katie Pasquini Masopust
(initial piece)

PHOTO BY HAWHORNE STUDIO

*Big Leaves,*
72" x 68",
by Katie Pasquini Masopust
(improved piece)

PHOTO BY HAWHORNE STUDIO

# Conclusion

Congratulations! Your toolbox is equipped! Keep adding to it. Remember what you learn, so you can use that information in your day-to-day life. You must continually feed your right brain with challenging exercises and projects. Right-brain stimulation is essential to your creative growth.

**Contour drawing** can be your way of doodling while on the phone or stuck in a waiting room. Look around, find something to **see**, and make **blind contour drawings** to keep your drawing skills strong. Notice the colors that are used in your favorite quilts and other art works. Did the artist use a full **value run**, a recognizable **color scheme**? Can you determine the **composition**? When you start a new project, decide whether you want to **free-cut** with fused fabrics or use **templates**. Continue to look for **inspiration** from photographs, magazine images, or your imagination. Keep a notebook of ideas, paint, sculpt, sing, dance, be creative in everything you do. Every experience done creatively uses the right side of the brain, and that is what keeps you open to artistic ideas.

As an artistic quilter, it is important for you to take classes (in quilting and other media), talk to your peers, and continue reading books. The idea of the solitary artist alone in a backwoods studio, slavishly producing piece after piece, is a myth. In today's society, interaction with new ideas and people is critical to your artistic evolution.

If you have created something from the exercises in this book, or if you have any questions, feel free to email us at (Katie) katiepm@aol.com or (Brett) artseegirl@msn.com.

PHOTO BY HAWTHORNE STUDIO

*Abiquiu Cliffs,* 30" x 45", painting by Brett Barker

# ABOUT THE AUTHORS

**Brett Barker and Katie Pasquini Masopust**

Fiber artist **Katie Pasquini** was born and raised in Eureka, California, with her seven brothers and sisters. She graduated from Eureka High School, where her main focus was the arts. After her senior year, Katie lived in Woodside, California, caring for her mother, who had Lou Gehrig's disease. While there, she attended a quilting class, which started Katie on her fantastic journey with cloth.

When Katie and her mom returned to Eureka, she opened Katie's Quilt Shop, which she ran for five years. She then began traveling in the United States, Canada, New Zealand, Australia, Japan, Belgium, Switzerland, and England, teaching contemporary quilt designing.

Katie has changed her style over the years, starting with traditional works, then creating mandalas, followed by dimensional quilts. She is enjoying landscapes and flora and feels as though she has returned full circle to her beginnings as a painter. Now she is painting with fabric.

Katie has won many awards throughout her career, including the Penny Nii award at the 1998 Visions Show for her quilt *Passages, Chaco Canyon.* Her quilt *Rio Hondo* was chosen as one of the 100 quilts of the twentieth century.

You can reach Katie Pasquini Masopust at
email: katiepm@aol.com
website: www.katiepm.com

**Brett Barker** first explored art as a teenager in Malmö, Sweden. She continued her studies while attending college in Claremont, California. While working in production at CBS Television, she often designed logos and graphics for various companies in the Los Angeles area. Finally, her desire to become a full-time artist and teacher could no longer be ignored, and she moved back to her native New Mexico, attending the University of New Mexico as a fine arts major. She opened her own studio in 1992, teaching art to children and adults. She continued painting and selling her art to collectors in the United States and Europe.

Brett now divides her time between teaching and creating art. Her business, Sun Studios Creativity Center, has reached quilters and other artists through the years. Her artwork can be seen in Santa Fe, New Mexico, and continues to be collected throughout the United States. In addition, Brett writes for the *SAQA Newsletter* and other artistic publications. She travels throughout the United States, teaching quilters and other artists to explore their creativity and expand their knowledge.

You can reach Brett Barker at
email: artseegirl@msn.com

**Other books by Katie Pasquini Masopust**

*Mandala: For contemporary quilt designs and other medium* and *The Contemporary Sampler,* both reprinted by Dover; *3 Dimensional Design, Isometric Perspective,* and *Fractured Landscapes* reprinted by Katie; and *Ghost Layers and Color Washes* published by C&T Publishing, Inc.

**For More Information**

Ask for a free catalog:
C&T Publishing, Inc.
P.O. Box 1456
Lafayette, CA 94549
800-284-1114
email: ctinfo@ctpub.com
website: www.ctpub.com

**Quilting Supplies**

Cotton Patch Mail Order
3404 Hall Lane
Dept. CTB
Lafayette, CA 94549
800-835-4418   925-283-7883
email: quiltusa@yahoo.com
website: www.quiltusa.com

NOTE: FABRICS USED IN THE QUILTS AND EXERCISES SHOWN MAY NOT BE CURRENTLY AVAILABLE BECAUSE FABRIC MANUFACTURERS KEEP MOST FABRICS IN PRINT FOR ONLY A SHORT TIME.

# INDEX

## Student Quilts

## Professional Works